MORE PRAISE FOR *WAKE UP*

"You've always had a wonderful, genial, wise voice and a gift for storytelling. Moreover this is a time when men need to hear from other men. You hear that all over the #metoo world. Men need to figure out the way to live in this changing world and they long to hear from other men. You are thoughtful and have the street cred to be the wise elder in a confusing time. The title is terrific."

—Ellen Goodman, Pulitzer Prize winning author and columnist

"John Spooner's written the ultimate road map so that men and women can arrive at their destination honorably—without even ignoring directions! Every man should inhale this book!"

—Lesley Visser, Hall of Fame broadcaster and sportswriter

"What a perfect time for a message some of us—yes, that would be the male of the species—don't like to hear: men can learn a lot from smart women. But delivered by John Spooner, a particularly insightful guide, this message goes down easily, lightly, with considerable humor and much charm. Who'd have guessed growing up would be such fun?"

—Margery Eagan, WGBH radio host and former *Boston Globe* columnist

"It's terrific. Informative, moving, and inspiring."

—William Phillips, former editor-in-chief, Little, Brown and Company Publishing

WAKE UP

N. SPOONER

WAKE UP:

A Lifetime of Lessons
from Smart Women

JOHN D. SPOONER

TidePool Press
Cambridge, Massachusetts

TidePool Press, LLC
6 Maple Avenue, Cambridge, Massachusetts 02139
www.tidepoolpress.com

Printed in the United States

Author's Disclaimer: All of the women in this book are real and their advice
priceless to me. They cover the spectrum of race, religion, and wisdom from the
actual worlds they inhabit. Some of them want to be anonymous and wish their
privacy to be respected. I have honored that. But their lessons to me make me
grateful every day. And have changed my life in countless ways.

Library of Congress Cataloging-in-Publication Data

John D. Spooner, 1937–
     Wake Up: A Lifetime of Lessons from Smart Women
     p.cm.
     978-1-7367720-8-9
     1. Spooner, John D.—memoir, biography 2. Gender studies
     3. Advice 4. Life Lessons
     I. Title.

     2 0 2 4 9 3 2 8 9 6

Cover design and illustration by Nicholas Spooner

For the women who have sustained and inspired my business life in so many ways. I'm so lucky to have you in my life: Bridget Basilico, Yvonne Russell and Felicia DiStasio.

And for my daughter Amanda ... my rock.

CONTENTS

A friend of mine at dinner once said to me:

"When I was six years old I had a red wagon. I was pulling it one day in front of my house with my friend, Margie, sitting in the wagon. My grandmother was visiting and came outside, watching me. 'You're going to hurt yourself,' she yelled, '*She* should be pulling *you*.'"

I never forgot that advice.

INTRODUCTION

This is women's time. I've been saying this to myself for the last few years. But now, every time I'm in a social gathering, I usually pound a few times with my palm on the table and say this out loud to get people's attention, and reinforce my own feelings.

How do I know that this is women's time? Because I'm a man who has benefited my entire life from the wisdom and practicality of many women. They have nurtured me, taught me, refined me when they thought I needed refining, pushed me into making important decisions, pointed my way at various crossroads. Some of them have even loved me.

I have had hundreds of women clients all over the world, of all ages and economic backgrounds. Strong women friendships as well, outside of my business life. Women are bedrock. More than ever they are providing advice and moral compass for me. Men need a lot of help. I think we were programmed to go out, kill the brontosaurus and bring back the steaks. That's not enough in this new era where there's such a blurring of traditional roles. I'm helped every day by women's advice. All men can be helped if they pay attention to the women in their lives. Men need to pay attention.

———

Only last week, a young woman in a new land reinforced several themes I keep absorbing. I never get tired of these original ways women present their wisdom, most of it street-smart. Their stories make me think and make me smile as well.

I was visiting a young friend in a rehab hospital. As I was leaving, I called Uber for a ride home. A young woman showed up in a black SUV. Her name jumped off the screen: "Blessing." She spoke with a little lilt to her voice. People interact with Uber drivers; everyone seems to act peer to peer. We're buddies. Blessing told me that she came from Uganda and arrived in Boston knowing nobody. No relatives here. Nothing.

"Usually, when people come to America, for the last 100 years, they have people from their home country to welcome them. Relatives," I said.

"Not me," she answered. "But a social worker knew how to ask questions to a smart phone, and she searched for Ugandan people in Boston. She found that Ugandans lived in Watertown, next to Cambridge, next to Boston. So I went to Watertown in a taxi and walked with my little suitcase on streets where there were shops and food markets and restaurants. No one looked like Ugandans. But, after walking and asking people on sidewalks, I saw a couple who looked like me. They even walked like Ugandans." She laughed as if she knew I couldn't possibly understand. "There are some things we can tell," Blessing said, "that you can't explain."

The Ugandans on the sidewalk gave her assistance and were kind. "But I asked them, first thing, something I knew would get me settled in America. I asked them, 'Where do Ugandans go to church? I'll go there. I can sing in choirs.'"

"Will you sing something for me?" I asked. Blessing sang a song in her language, a language I do not understand. She said it was a hymn, and her voice was lovely.

"What's the message in the song?" I asked. She looked over her shoulder briefly, as we were going over a bridge.

"It says that there *is* a God."

She told me that she had four children who were back in Uganda, cared for by her mother. And that she was married for ten years.

"Is their father in the picture?" I asked.

"He's useless," she said. "He used to steal our money to drink and gamble. He shows up now. But not for the children, only when he wants something. He is father to them all."

"Well," I said, "you must have loved him for *at least* four years. Why did you stay with him?" Again she looked over her shoulder. "Because every night I went to bed I thought it would be better tomorrow."

Blessing lives in a group home and takes care of the people in residence. She drives for Uber to bring in extra money. "I've learned, too," she said, "that nice people I meet can maybe lead me to different jobs, a different life. Do you know 'Amazing Grace?'"

"I do," I said. "Kind of … "

I sang with her the rest of the way to my home and exchanged cards when we parted. "Bless you," she said, as I climbed out of the car, but not before I reached over and shook her hand. Who could ever resist a blessing from a Blessing?

———

Susan, my wife of forty-five years, died of lung cancer in June 2011. We were all alone in our house, looking out of our bedroom at sailboats, white against blue, rushing into harbor. "It's late, isn't it?" she asked, coming in and out of morphine-assisted sleep. Those were her last words to me.

Susan was the adult in our house. She was the most honest person I've ever known, comfy in her skin, not afraid to say *"no"* to our children, to invitations that I thought would enhance our social status, to club memberships in faraway locations. When occasionally I seemed to be going off the rails on some madcap schedule, she'd arch one eyebrow and say, after a pause, "Grow up." I repeat that to myself a lot, with her sitting on my shoulder. It helps me be honest with myself. She was funny too, in her honesty. Years before she was diagnosed with cancer, she gave me a list of names at our nightly cocktail time. There were five names of women on it. "What's this?" I asked her.

"If anything ever happens to me," she said, "none of these dames gets to go anywhere near my closet." She did have great clothes and I understand all of the implications in her tone: "Don't try to BS me."

In the 1970s as the women's liberation movement emerged, more and more people would say to each other, when meeting for the first time, "And what do *you* do?" Susan had a modeling career at a high level in our city, but gave it up to be home, running the household and raising three children. To her it was a noble calling and typical for much of our generation. She resented the implication that what she did was becoming somehow not worthy. At parties when she was asked the inevitable question, particularly by men, "What do *you* do?," she would answer, "I'm a brain surgeon, specializing in the prefrontal lobes of immature men." It always led to laughter, and eventual friendship. "Always try to be a surprise to people," she said. I've taken that lesson to heart over the years. But I'm always aware that it has to be coupled with her warning that I *grow up!*

The first New Year's Eve I spent alone since we had dated, was in 2012. That night, I was invited to dinner at an old friend's apartment in Boston, only about a mile from where I live, a walkable distance on the chilly, clear night. There is a grand fireworks display every New Year's Eve on Boston Common, where cows grazed during Revolutionary times. It has been estimated that as many as one million people pour into the city to watch the show and stay for First Night festivities; mostly free performances for all the family, all over the city. I walked from my house, two blocks to Charles Street, a long thoroughfare bisecting the Common from the Public

Garden, hundreds of thousands of celebrators streaming towards the fireworks site. I said to myself, "How typical of my life, everyone moving toward the brilliant explosions. And me, moving in the opposite direction," even thinking, "I care much more about watching people's faces than seeing the sky lit up by fire." The loneliness wrapped around me like a scarf. We were married for a long time. But if anything is ever good in life, it's never long enough.

I rejected all the clichés like, "She's in a better place." I don't think so. Or "Life goes on." I say, "define life." Of course, I was feeling sorry for myself and not proud of it. The crowd pushed against me, families oohing and aahing with every explosion of sparkling lights, excited by the show, warmed in the freezing night, staying close to strangers.

Later that winter, I went to a birthday party for a high school classmate. One of the guests was a man, a doctor with the reputation of being "the best internist in Boston; smart and caring." I knew that he had lost his wife some years before and had remarried. After dinner, he came up to me and said, "I'm so sorry about Susan. Of course we had heard. If you don't mind I'd like to tell you a little story."

"Sure," I answered.

"After my first wife died," the doctor said, "it was obviously very hard. And then I threw myself into work, buried myself in it. One day a patient came in to see me, an older Italian woman who still spoke with an accent after years in this country and always wore a black dress. She gave me her condolences, went through her examination, then left. About ten minutes later she appeared in the office again.

"'Just a minute more of your time, please,' she said. 'Something I forgot.'

"She came in and asked me to sit down and I did. She stared at me for some time and then said, 'I thought you should hear this. *She's not coming back.*' Then she got up, pressed my hands briefly in hers. And left."

My initial reaction to what the Italian woman said was that I wished the doctor had not told me that story. I didn't want to hear anyone say that "she's not coming back." Of course, the message she was passing on to him and by extension to me was one of understanding. The Italian woman counseled the internist. By proxy, she counseled me. But you have to be ready for messages, and often have to step back to appreciate the words in full. She knew that I had to climb back on the bicycle of living.

I've been learning lessons from women all of my life ... I grew up in my maternal grandparents' house, during the days alone with three women for my first five years, my grandmother, my mother and Katie, the Irish cook who worked for the family for over 53 years. Growing up I thought these three women did everything. The men, my grandfather and father, were gone all day, and I had no idea what they did. And no one ever told me. So early on I got the sense that life was run by the women, and that men went out and did stuff that really wasn't very interesting, or else they would talk about it at home.

How early can you learn about love? My grandparents were immigrants from Eastern Europe, a little town outside of Kraków, Poland, a village in fact, right out of *Fiddler on the Roof*. Grandpa did want to become rich, like Tevye, when he arrived in Boston in 1895. He and many of his friends had one passionate desire, to become really American as fast as they could. He threw himself into activities, particularly sports. Specifically baseball. He was a tough little catcher in the Boston League on the Boston Common. He also worked from the time he was seven, living in a three-room apartment with his parents and four siblings. They had a bathtub. But the family never used it. It was where they stored the coal for heating. He also boxed professionally in his late teens, under the name, "Kid Manning," because most of the boxers, also immigrant kids, were Irish.

Eventually he went into the manufacturing business; maternity underwear, mainly slips. The business prospered. He married, and my grandparents had four children, three boys and my mother. My immigrant grandparents built a big brick house outside the city, right next to Boston College. The area was basically Yankee paradise, and my family was among the first Jewish newcomers to this bastion of old Brahmin families. Like them, they hired Irish immigrants to work in their houses. Katherine Faherty came into my family's lives when she was 18.

Katie was a philosopher. When faced with a problem she would always say, "God is good and Jack is fishing," meaning that Jack would be successful if he believed.

Katie had the knack for love and the gift of laughter. She arrived from Connemara, County Galway, after World War I, her only possession a gold sovereign dated 1907 with a glorified likeness of Edward VII on one side, St. George and the dragon on the other.

In this house, Katie learned to cook the dishes of Eastern Europe and Russia. People came from towns away, from states away, to taste Katie's gefilte fish, matzoh balls, chopped liver, potato pancakes, cherry cheesecake. Katie got at least two offers a week from families holding out to her bigger houses, bigger rooms, more pay, more vacation, other than the typical Thursday and Sundays, after lunch had been served.

Katie helped raise my mother and uncles and, when they were grown, she raised me. I was born there, my parents living also in the big brick house. I was Katie's boy, somehow singled out by her to be Irish, despite my Eastern European forebears. She educated me in the songs and stories of Galway. I could sing, "Whiskey, You're the Devil" before I could sing "America the Beautiful." Katie used to sit me in my highchair in the middle of the kitchen floor singing, "Me mother sent me out to France, to learn the steps of the fogie dance," and she'd do the village dance, punctuating it with her own drum solos, spoons on saucepans, carving knife on crystal glasses.

The radio played *The Irish Hour* in the kitchen for me and her friends who worked in the neighborhood and came over to gossip about dances at Hibernian Hall in Roxbury, about boat trips to the old country, five-dollar bills sent home to the family, deaths of siblings, always deaths.

Every week the phone calls came when my immigrant grandmother was out. "Katie, come make chopped liver for us, stuffed derma for us, cheesecake. You want $60 a week, saints days off? You tell us." She always resisted. Because it wasn't money that made life bearable. It was loyalty and passion and a sense of one's center. No free-agent status for Katie. She was committed to family and committed to love.

Unlike so many modern parents, Katie demanded excellence. Because she gave it, she assumed it was essential in others. She was profane if you didn't measure up to her standards. I tutored her in her exam for citizenship. "You didn't read it right," she would scold.

Many times she took me to St. Ignatius Church at Boston College, leaving me to brood in dark silence at the stained glass, sailing paper boats in the font of holy water. Over the years Archbishop (later Cardinal) Cushing would be there. "Katie," he would scold. "I know he's taken Communion dozens of times. This is a Jewish boy." The archbishop was always gentle. He knew Katie was the best cook in Boston.

"It doesn't matter, your Excellency," Katie would insist. "Ask him yourself … he's Irish in his heart." I thought I was, too.

In the summers my grandparents moved my family to Nantasket Beach, to a summer house on Boston's South Shore. Next door lived Bernard Goldfine, a textile manufacturer. Goldfine was a power broker who threw a medicine ball back and forth in the driveway every morning with his chauffeur. He also pulled political strings for his benefit, raising money to keep cronies in power, sprinkling gifts and cash. Katie would take me up to her room at night to sit on her bed and watch through the window into Goldfine's dining room where Governor Paul Dever, Mayor John Hynes and Ambassador Joe Kennedy often gathered. "Be quiet and listen," Katie would say. "You'll learn what to do when you're a man and knowing secrets." I could hear them through the screens.

When Katie died she was surrounded by generations of people who loved her, who knew her wit, her chopped liver, her Toll House cookies, her songs from home. I was there too. She had bought me the first *Superman* and *Captain Marvel* comic books and told me "Save these. They'll be worth a lot of money someday." She would spend her dimes for the comics, hiding them for me in a pantry drawer. How many people do you know who are both the best cook in Boston and the best investment advisor? "God is good and Jack is fishing."

When I was 21, Katie gave me her gold coin with the English king on one side. I had it attached to a thin gold chain, which I wear in honor of her, on every St. Patrick's Day. She taught me, beyond anything else, that it is possible to offer unconditional love.

I'm in a people business, managing more than a billion-and-a-half dollars of client money, counseling them on so many issues that go way beyond their involvement with stocks and bonds.

I can play golf with the guys, swap jokes and travel stories, shoot the breeze about past adventures and who they see for orthopedic problems. But when I need advice about how the world works, and how you survive the bumps … I talk to women.

Men should be taught about the things that really matter. It can help their careers and their relationships.

We need a lot of help.

1 | MINDS OF THE MILLENIALS

Allison runs six miles a day, six times a week. She's 27 years old and works for a startup in Boston, focusing on cybersecurity. She's a fellow trustee on the board of the *Harvard Lampoon*, the oldest college humor magazine in America, founded in 1876.

My favorite people in the world, my closest friends, female and male, are what I call "bent." It's a compliment. To me, "bent" means people who always wondered when they were little, why they felt different from the other kids. Bent people are the grit in the oyster; the round peg in the square hole.

When I was a rookie on the *Lampoon* board, I knew no one. When I was on the magazine in college, all of the writers wanted to write the Great American Novel. John Updike was one of them; he did it with *Rabbit Run*. Today the emphasis is on television comedy: *Saturday Night Live, The Simpsons, Veep* and endless others.

I still vote for the novel. But Allison rolls on, taking it all in at the meetings, observing. She's the novelist in the crowd, if she had that itch. But she doesn't yet.

If you manage people's money, you have to understand human nature. You have to understand what the different generations care about, from the baby boomers to the millennials and beyond.

"I majored in English," Allison told me, "and didn't write a thesis. But I did co-write a book parody of the movie, *Hunger Games*, called *Hunger Pains* that was a commercial success."

After I knew her for a while I asked her, "Why didn't you go West, into television comedy?"

"By some miracle," she said, "I came out of college with no debt, but I had no trust fund, no slush fund. I went to work a week after I graduated college. The company was Hungry Fish Media," she told me, "they needed a copywriter and I figured I could do that. The company sold nutritional supplements, online vitamins. I had no idea what I was going to do with my life, no dream to be an orthopedic surgeon or anything. I'd just figure it out.

"After a year I took an internship in Brazil. Brazil was booming; the BRIC countries were the hottest investments in the world then: Brazil, Russia, India and China. My company was the Weight Watchers of Brazil. They sold muscle-building supplements. I was working on mobile apps for them, a stranger in a strange land."

Allison came back to Boston from Brazil. "It would have been easy to go into consulting. Every big firm visited our college and threw offers at us. We didn't have to interview anywhere. Some people told me I was a natural for marketing. I somehow thought that marketing was making something *more* than it really was. If I worked for a company, I had to believe that it was doing a *service*."

Her generation raves about honesty, authenticity. Often, they seem to be migrants, looking for a tent over their heads, as they change jobs, see the world. But Allison is bent. She does have the soul of a novelist, taking it all in, here ... but also not here, the observer.

"I kind of backed into my niche at my current job," she says, "a startup specializing in cybersecurity. My focus has become new ideas for products, a product manager. My generation tends to switch jobs a lot. I see a lot of resumes and when I see one from a job jumper, I hesitate to hire them. Because I can never tell if they can work through the tough stuff. I think that we need to learn to work with people we don't like."

"Where'd you ever learn that?" I asked.

"Strangely enough," Allison said, "I learned it competing to get onto the *Lampoon*. The competition didn't involve being paddled like in *Animal House*. But the members brutalized you intellectually, particularly a couple of people. All the candidates were broken down in morality and decency. It was nihilism to the max. If you cared about *anything*, they'd break you. I powered through the rough stuff, and eventually figured out that they loved it if you survived. The more you persevered, the more they accepted you. They'd actually be kinder and gentler to the people they couldn't stand, in a funny way. Television comedy writing and producing was on their minds. They could win Emmys. I was one of the crowd, all of us loners in a pack. I went to an all-girls' Catholic high school in Rhode Island. What planet did I land on?"

She went on. "I was curious about what people wanted, what the customer wants. If I worked for a company, I had to believe in it, believe that it was doing a service."

"Could you be a CEO?" I asked her.

"Yes," she said. "But I'd worry about everybody's lives. I'd take it personally."

"Give me an idea of who your clients are."

"Small businesses," she said, "from 200 to 1,000 employees, like a specialty law firm who needs to protect confidential information, or a school district. I sell them our software, almost always online or on the phone. My job after the initial sale is to get the new client (and the old ones too) to add on software as they get comfortable with us to further protect their business. The add-ons are where the juice is."

Allison has given me several tips about protecting my own personal information and identity:

1. Get a shredder, or use your office shredder. Get in the habit of shredding everything that is on paper that could be used to hack you. It's sad, but you should make it a habit, like your sit-ups or calling your mother; part of your routine.

2. Any online questionnaire you get about passwords that ask "your mother's maiden name" or "the name of your first pet … " never answer these questionnaires. Cyber thieves are increasingly smart. They Google you. They know your habits. They have become behavioral scientists. They can know you better than *you* know you.

"We have zero privacy today, it seems," I told Allison. "Friends in the investment business tell me that their firms Google them to find out if they have outside activities they haven't told the firm. One of my friends has a client whose name was searched also by his firm and up popped the info that the client was wanted for grand larceny, and my friend was grilled about it. The real crook had the same name as the client, zero relation to one another. My friend said, 'Are we are all guilty until proven innocent?'"

Allison laughed. "Well, cybersecurity fits right in here. Cyber is always a trade-off. Do you want security or convenience? Where on the spectrum do you fall? Do you want discounts on merchandise of all kinds that you get if you cough up all sorts of information? It's a trade-off." She has a few suggestions for help.

1. Get a password manager, something that can help you with password choices and the tricks to keep your information safe. Last Pass is one of the sites you can search.

2. What you want to protect is basically credit cards and

bank accounts. Check them once a week to make sure there's no funny business.

3. Put a credit freeze on your accounts through Equifax. It prevents anyone tampering with your information.

4. "I go to 'black hat' conferences," she says, "to pick up tricks of the trade, to build the new relationships and learn about the competition. Companies should look into 'penetration testing.' There are firms you can hire whose job it is to *try* to hack you, to show you what you must do to prevent it. I've seen examples of hackers who come to offices disguised as pizza delivery men. They will wander around, listening to small talk, hoping to get information about the habits of the workers. Even the trash you toss out can be rifled for receipts. Several of my friends have been hacked, and they think it's from the green trash bags left outside for garbage pickup. People are sloppy about what and how they dispose of things."

Allison tells me that most of her best friends are men and that virtually all of the engineers at her job are men as well. "So many of them cry on my shoulder," she says. "They want advice about their careers, their love lives. They know I'll listen to them and they can't seem to talk to other men about problems. This is what I call 'emotional labor.' I think women are much better listeners." Allison rents an apartment in Boston with two male roommates. "I found them on Craigslist," she told me.

"One of the many things that's so different about your generation," I said. "After college I never wanted roommates ever again. I want privacy and space. And I'd *never* rent with people I didn't know."

Alison smiled as if I didn't have a clue. "Well, there's a lot of knocks on us, and misconceptions too. One of them seems to be that we have no plans for the future and want pleasure *now*, not deferred. I choose to have roommates because, while doing so, I can *save* $2,000 a month, save and invest. I want a place of my own, that I can *buy*, not rent. This is part of my plan ... Secure my future. Don't fiddle while Rome burns. Be smart about yourself.

"One big thing these days I advise men to do ... and it would work for men of *all* ages," she says, "spend a day trying to *think* like a woman. I believe an exercise like this would open a lot of men's eyes and improve their relationships, at work *and* at play." I asked Allison for her take on relationships, and if she had any specific advice for young men *and* women about their future.

"Sure," she says, in no particular order:

1. Don't be afraid to get out of comfort zones. I work with engineers all the time and I've never taken a science course in my life. But I've learned to understand software.

2. Design your career choices so that you're not working 90 hours a week.

3. For dating, I do prefer Tinder to other sites. I'm attracted to men who have strong interests other than mine, and they must have a direction in their career. Partially so I can learn new things from them. But mostly because I believe a long-term relationship can only be sustained by each partner having areas they can retreat into that gives them some space and satisfaction.

4. I think my age cohort who seem who seem obsessed with traveling the world would be well-served by seeing America. Our own country is really many countries, and it would serve my generation well if they explored it and opened themselves up to the unexpected.

5. There are times you cannot afford to seem to be needy.

When I meet new people, or have potential clients come into my office, I ask them, "What's your favorite all-time book?" It's a quick character study. I believe you can learn a lot about someone by their answer to that question.

Without hesitation Allison said, "Well, mine is *Moby-Dick*."

"That's a surprise," I said.

She smiled, "*Moby-Dick* is so surprising *itself*, particularly how much humor is in the novel. It's about *everything*."

Allison always reinforces a lesson I've tried to absorb all my life. *Try to be a surprise to people.*

SPEND A DAY TRYING TO THINK LIKE A WOMAN.

2 | GOLF LESSONS: BOYS AND GIRLS

You can learn a lot about human nature on a golf course. Over almost a five-hour 18-hole round, it's a wonderful character study. You find out about your companion's interests, their family, what matters to them. You also discover if they're good sports, if they're honorable, if they cheat. It's so much more than "a good walk spoiled" by the difficulty of the game.

It's also full of lessons about the differences between men and women and how men's lives can be improved by paying attention to these differences.

I played nine holes in a men's foursome recently, and I took notes on what we discussed during the round. I did not initiate any of the subjects, merely reacted to what others brought up.

We talked about the US open at Shinnecock on Long Island, and if Tiger Woods would ever win again. We talked about real estate prices and if there was a bubble in Boston housing. Several dirty jokes were told, there is always *someone* in a men's foursome who tells dirty jokes. We talked about the weather in the freezing winter and spring. We talked about the sponginess of certain holes, the lack of drainage, and the pitiful shape of the sand in the bunkers.

We watched a blue heron cruise into a pond landing and remarked on the beauty of that, and one of our foursome told us about having to stop his car while a pair of wild turkeys led ten babies across the road while he waited. "Like at a pedestrian crossroad," he said. We never talked about one thing that was personal in their lives, except one man complaining about how many children and grandchildren were going to visit for the weekend. It was kind of a grumpy tour, missed shots, missed putts, enjoying the day, but kind of an "arm's length" experience.

Did I learn anything useful from my two hours with the boys? I learned that no one talked about anything really personal in two hours except health issues.

A week later I was with a different foursome, playing with one of my best friends, an usher in our wedding. He talked with me about one of his loves: reading. We swapped book recommendations. The other two men were new to me. One talked about his business before he retired and we played, "Do you know so-and-so?" I like that game, particularly when it turns out that you have many people in common. He was a wonderful player. It's a pleasure to watch anyone play a sport at a high level, something most of us can only dream about. The other man has been on Wall Street. "I used to be somebody," he told me. He complained almost the whole day about "how the business has changed, how boring the people in the business were. No characters anymore; the fun left Wall Street years ago."

We all love stories. There was action involved as well. Most men play golf with something on the line. They play for money. It can be for small amounts, where you could win or lose five or six dollars. Or the stakes could go up to the hundreds for the match. In some crowds, it can be multiples of that. There is even a betting game on the course called "skins." The guys often want to have "skin in the game."

There's an old phrase about the sport ... "Golf is the only thing you'll ever do in your life, where you get what you deserve." I believe it.

My friend Dorothy is a superb athlete, a natural. Many good athletes have the skills for it, but not the brain. Dorothy can think around a tennis court and a golf course, when to lob, when to attack the net, when to lay up in golf, and when to go for it.

For some time, Dorothy was on the board of the LPGA. She officiated at women's tournaments all over the country, an expert on the rules of golf. My wife loved Dorothy. But she would say, "I won't play with her. She'll never even give me a six-inch putt. It's no fun unless I can take two swings at every shot and kick it out of the woods."

She was kidding. But also serious. Golf for her was a laugh, a good walk. But never spoiled because it was the companionship of women that made her love the sport. As long as it occasionally included a legitimate par.

I asked several of my women golfer friends to do what I did, take notes on what their foursomes talked about over their nine-hole game. Completely different conversations. The women I spoke with were of various ages, sharing a love of golf for different reasons. One thing Dorothy always does. She puts every putt in the hole. She never accepts "that's good," and picks the ball up. She'll play by the rules of golf, "Put every putt in the hole, even if it's two inches," she tells me. "That's how the game should be played." I hear this from women players of every ability, from single digit handicap golfers, to weekend women who want to do it right. One of my aunts, a good player, said to me, "I bet if every man played by the true rules of golf, most of them couldn't honestly break 100." She might have been kidding, but I could never really tell.

As for conversation, the women I polled told me, "In matches, we're serious. We concentrate on the game and the competition."

In friendly rounds the topics ranged from job stories, health stories, including doctor recommendations, books, children, husband's behavior, including some sexual stories that were personal. (Men talk about sex in jokes, almost never personal tales.) Women also talked politics in those casual games and tips on making daily lives easier, what apps they used, what products. Men never really talked about anything personal, and seldom asked advice from their fellow players about anything, even stock ideas.

Most women use the outings for mutual reassurance, for information, and yes, gossip too. But they were never islands alone the way the men were. Women's islands were populated with all aspects of life. Men pushed their carts, or rode in them, or walked with caddies, or carried their own bags. All of them single soldiers, not a team.

The same sport, but different reasons for playing.

TRY LETTING OUT A SOFTER SIDE THAT NO ONE EXPECTS. IF YOU SHOW A LITTLE VULNERABILITY, WHAT YOU HEAR BACK CAN BE VERY USEFUL. AND PUT EVERY PUTT IN THE HOLE.

3 | ADVICE FROM OLDER WOMEN

I'm not sure why I've always been attracted to strong independent women, women who had to carry the load, who always knew they were different, no matter the roles that society thought they should be occupying.

My Aunt Marsha was a key person in my life. She taught me how to tie my shoelaces when I was three, one of the few mechanical skills I've mastered over the years. No one else in the family would've thought of this, much less have the patience to stick it out until it took.

"There's nothing more ridiculous than a little boy tripping over his laces," she said. "You want to have people laughing with you, not *at* you." She would repeat this to me over the years.

I remember sitting on the floor in my grandfather's house, Aunt Marsha next to me, technical advisor to little me in my Stride Rites.

She looked to me like a Viking princess. I was the only child in the house of five adults and no little children on our street to play with. The men in the house taught me to throw and catch a baseball and how to ride a bike. The women taught me how to deal with life issues. Everything else I learned, in my friendless first five years, I absorbed from books, and the illustrations and photos in those books, *Grimm's Fairy Tales*, stories of maidens and knights.

Later on, visiting with my parents in Aunt Marsha's house, she taught me about painters, particularly van Gogh, Matisse, Monet, whose prints, cut from magazines and framed, she hung on her walls. "Don't be boring," she would tell me, "use both sides of your brain. Practical side, yes … but travel, take art lessons, go to concerts. See Monet's house in Giverny, steal a pebble from the garden for me. Steal two and carry one around with you for luck. Have a soft side; the hard-ass part of being a man is crap. Particularly if you ever want an interesting woman in your life." I remember about this time, at a family dinner, when she announced, "I'm running off with Ezio Pinza." Pinza was a star opera singer at the time, the male lead in Rodgers and Hammerstein's *South Pacific*. "He's my kind of guy." She didn't actually pursue him. But, at the time, I thought she was capable of anything. All of this she offered when I was 12, 13, 14. My first plane flight ever was to London when I had graduated from college. Eighteen hours. But I had been fully armed by Aunt Marsha to "look at life from both sides now."

But the best life advice I ever got from her was when I was hearing from colleges and making a decision. *Life* magazine, when I was growing up, was America's television long before TV. From age three on, I couldn't wait to see the photographs that poured off the pages of *Life*. One week in the early 1950s they did a photo spread on Williams College. It seemed magical to me, set on a New England *Our Town* campus, everyone looking to me, incredibly perfect. But it somehow seemed a place of excellence. I had my sights and heart set on it. There were no early admissions then, not much help from any school counselors or faculty at big public high schools. Zero help from parents, who never went to any games we played (we didn't want them there anyway). There were no back-to-school nights. Many of the parents were first-generation Americans.

I got into Williams College and was all set to accept. I had also gotten into Harvard. Aunt Marsha was always so very *sure* about everything. Her likes and dislikes were always on display, with a loud voice that seemed to me to blow away any dissent.

"Harvard's so huge," I said.

"Your parents have wrapped you in cotton," she said. "You'll have about three major crossroads in life. This is one of them and you want to be smart about it. Smart can lead to *luck*. You cannot turn down Harvard. And here's my other big tip to you. When you enroll in a really big school, find some way to make it *small*. Go out for a sport, join the Spanish club, write for the newspaper, audition for a play. Throw yourself into something that shrinks the place. That's where you'll find your true home in college."

First week Freshman year at Harvard, I went out for lightweight crew, having never seen a crew shell before. I barely made the team, the last man on the squad, a perpetual "extra." But the friendships made there literally changed my life, opening doors for me I could never have imagined.

And eventually, years later, I visited Giverny, Monet's home, and took back two stones, one for me and one for Aunt Marsha.

TRY TO MAKE A BIG PLACE SMALL.

24

4 | YOU'LL NEVER FORGET ME

If we're lucky in life, we know people in their eighties or older who seem younger than people in their forties. Such a person is my friend Sylvia. It's an old-fashioned name, but she's more modern and original in my view than Lady Gaga. I've had a crush on Sylvia for a long time, dating back to when I was a junior counselor at a boys' camp in Maine and her son was in my charge. This was long before the concept of the "cougar." But like Jimmy Carter, I lusted in my heart. Sylvia was an extreme redhead, in the mode of Maureen O'Hara in the great movie, with John Wayne as her costar, *The Quiet Man.*

Years later, we became friends when she was working in the retail business. "I can sell more clothes than anyone in this store," she told me, "because I'm good to people. I'm interested in them and their stories. When you get people to talk about themselves, they will buy much more than they thought they would. If you're a good listener, you can be a great salesperson." She also taught me to "keep relationships and friendships fresh." She does this by sending little notes with thoughts on life. Some of her notes have read, "I'm looking for a dirty old man with a clean body." And "most of the frogs you kiss never turn into princes." *Her* lines, not the sappy print in the cards.

"To get somewhere in life," she said, "you have to make yourself memorable." Some years ago, she came into my office wearing a painted wooden sign around her neck that read, "Be Good To Me, I'm Old." Another time, she wore dark glasses and held a tin cup in her hands full of sharpened No. 2 pencils. Next to her, she'd placed a stuffed toy dog with a silver chain around its neck wearing dark glasses. "I won't have to sell pencils, will I?" she asked sheepishly. Stock markets had been soft and anxious, and Sylvia wanted to make sure I was paying attention to her and her money.

For a famous psychiatrist friend's birthday, Sylvia bought a large glass head, open at the top. She filled it with nuts and presented it to him. "They're all nuts," she would say. "Ever know kids who had a shrink for a dad? I rest my case." For a favorite cousin's anniversary, she bought a whole cooked tongue (her cousin's favorite food), at a kosher butcher shop. Then Sylvia put together a papier-mâché head, complete with mop strings for hair and a generously wide mouth, into which she placed the deli tongue, sticking out grotesquely. "Keep 'em guessing what's next," she advised me, adding, "I don't know about you, but I've put in my will that I want my ashes scattered somewhere in Neiman Marcus. To be eternally aware of when they run the sales."

Sylvia had just turned 95 years old. She wasn't walking so well, but she visited my office, accompanied by a younger friend of hers who helped her over the rough spots. "This is Anne," Sylvia said, introducing us. "I've known her since she was 17 or 18, when she was in college, working part-time at Filene's." Sylvia also introduced me to a stuffed toy ostrich, which Anne wheeled in, strapped to something that resembled a skateboard. Anne also carried in a shiny aluminum bucket. In the bucket was a velvet bag, full of something that felt, as I hefted it, to be squishy.

"What's all this, Sylvia?" I asked her. She always had stories, and she usually had punchlines to go with them. I think that if she had been born 20 years later than she was, she would have run an advertising agency. Or been a stand up comedienne in the mode of Phyllis Diller or Joan Rivers.

"Well," she said to me, "I haven't looked at my brokerage statement in a year. My head's in the sand. Like this ostrich." The black bag in the bucket was full of sand. There was a label on the outside. It read, "Gucci."

When Sylvia had gone to the ladies room on that day, Anne smiled at me. "Never knew anyone like her. I knew nothing about anything when I was at UMass. She educated me; I went to *her* graduate school. One day I told her I had fallen in love with a pair of shoes. 'But they cost two weeks pay,' I told Sylvia.

"'Just buy them,' Sylvia said. 'Indulge yourself. One of my rules is: Don't look back at something you wanted; a trip, a romance, a special pair of shoes. Work harder, overtime, whatever it takes. Dare to do it. For instance,' Sylvia went on, 'years ago, I was a young married woman, my husband working in a family business. He squeezed the nickels, if you know what I mean. Well, I saw these thigh-high boots with big heels that were a fortune then, 500 bucks. He would've blown a gasket if I bought them, and I couldn't hide the bill because in those days, the husband paid the bills, and I wasn't working yet. But I had a plan. I bought the boots, put them on and was in the kitchen at the sink when he came home from work.' Sylvia paused a beat. 'But that's *all* I had on,' she said. 'My husband *never* mentioned the bill he eventually got.'

"Eventually," Anne also told me, "I married, had children, and my husband and I did well. We bought a rather large house, with seven bathrooms. When Sylvia visited, she said, 'Who can pee in all these bathrooms?' A day later, a FedEx arrived; the package was huge and contained two white trash bags, tied up with white satin ribbons. Both bags were *full* of toilet paper rolls."

She went on. "Sylvia took me to the theater when I had never been to a theater. And the symphony too. She taught me then. She still teaches me. The tricks of the trade I've learned, all came from her taking the time to teach a kid. Thank God, now I can take *her* to the theater.

"Every time I think of her, I smile."

THERE ARE TIMES TO BE OUTRAGEOUS.

5 | GIRLS' NIGHT OUT

In every city I've visited in this country in the last several years, on any given night in restaurants, I've seen two women having dinner together. Four women, six women, eight women, all totally engaged in conversation, laughing, into each other. Several times I've gone over to them, excused myself, and mentioned that I was working on a book focused on the lessons women could teach men. Instantly, they all wanted to hear more, so I told them how many women had educated and nurtured me, from the time I was an infant. I asked each of these groups, "How many different subjects do you typically discuss at the dinners you have?"

Universally, almost all of them mentioned the following, in no special order: children, books, volunteerism, job opportunities, aging parents, unruly siblings, politics, healthcare, including tips on doctors and their specialties, pets, beauty aids, exercise regimes.

Husbands and boyfriends were down around the bottom of these lists.

Almost always I ask the group, "How come there is no such thing as 'boys' night out?'" I get the same answer, with different phrasing, every time. The women would laugh. They'd look at each other in knowing ways, and one of them would say, "Because they're clueless." In my experience, this seems to be a consensus. What about anything that passes for boys' night out? This seems to boil down to two gatherings. One is going to games. In Boston, it's our teams; Red Sox, Bruins, Celtics, Patriots. On these outings, it's almost completely sports talk. What the guys played in high school (the glory days), college, tales from the past about famous Boston triumphs or disasters, more high school stuff ("Remember when?" Or, "Whatever happened to Lefty?" Or, "My dream was to date a drum majorette."). If you kick it up a notch, the guys will talk about deals, business, very little of a personal nature is discussed. *Show no weakness.* Go out and kill the brontosaurus; bring home the steaks.

In restaurants, periodically, you'll see a table of men in suits and open neck shirts, no ties. They can be beefy, loud and boisterous, if it's holiday season. The boys from the office. In this crowd, there will always be one or two women, joining in the gaiety. And you know it will be as buddies in the financial arena. If it's a giant group, seemingly led by one or two people, it will be a group of rookies, entertained by a manager or two, the rookies worried about keeping their jobs and how they would be rich someday.

Girls' night out is for therapy first, friendship second. Boys' night out is about the past and about who may be the lead dog.

Because I talk to women when they're on girls' night out, I get tips all the time on things that make my life better: their favorite doctors and dentists, what soaps and lotions I can use on my skin, who are the best exercise trainers, what new restaurants are interesting, books I might enjoy, movies worth seeing. Women get personal, they're consumers. They share secrets about people, places and things. Women can tell us things that are practical and useful.

Maybe you can educate your guy friends to make a more personal approach to problems of all kinds.

IMPROVE YOUR PERSONAL LIVES, GUYS.
PAY ATTENTION TO GIRLS' NIGHT OUT.

6 | FINDING YOUR VOICE AND USING IT

Much of what happens to us in life is not planned. It happens by accident. My friend Margaret doesn't seem like the image of a Margaret at all. Margaret, to me, sounds formal. I think of a nun, Sister Margaret. Others have agreed with me. She seems to have many nicknames; Buttercup, Peach, Mort, Maggie, or just plain M. She chaired the Henry R. Luce Foundation in New York, almost a billion dollar enterprise, founded by Henry R. Luce, the business genius who invented *Time* magazine and *Life*, which then led to *Fortune*, *People*, *Sports Illustrated*. But her day job was advertising, where she started as a secretary, making $12,000 a year and eating baked potatoes for dinner.

She never went to graduate school, but learned in what may be the best way, "on the job training."

"I moved little by little up the ladder," Margaret told me. "But I never really made a breakthrough until I was maybe 30, and I had a new direct report to a woman who I thought humorless. She watched me closely in several meetings with the CEO.

"'I have a suggestion for you,' the boss told me, 'you sit there and listen and take notes. You'll also ask questions. What you *want* to do is come in with *ideas*, not questions. You have to make it easier for the CEO. He doesn't want you coming in parroting others, he wants you to speak up, to relieve some of *his* stress. You're not being bossy, just showing that you're interested in enhancing the business. People can disagree with you, that's fine. But you're doing yourself a disservice by just sitting and taking notes.'"

Margaret told me that this insight completely changed the way she looked at her job. The advice moved her up the company food chain to more and more responsible duties and ultimately helped get her board positions in *both* the for-profit and nonprofit worlds.

Her advice I've passed on to many younger men seeking my advice. And I took it to heart myself. It's forced me to be more productive, particularly in meetings where I dreaded going. Once a year I write to the CEO of our firm in New York. Margaret's advice was so right. Many people in meetings, particularly in the investment business, voice complaints and/or ask questions. I'll offer several ideas in my letter, that I hope will *add* to productivity. The CEO always answers me in thoughtful ways and I know he finds ideas that are provocative to be helpful. Just the act of letter writing ... with *ideas*, keeps me on his radar and personalizes our relationship, even though it's long distance.

COME TO MEETINGS WITH IDEAS,
NOT QUESTIONS OR COMPLAINTS.

7 | ROMANCE AND THE TRAIN TEST

There was a famous bar in Harvard Square in Cambridge called The Casablanca, affectionately called, "The Casa B". You didn't want to see it in the daylight, a serious, dimly lit bar, that, for a long time had wicker seats for two; a padded cushion with a wicked wicker overhang that covered two people, like a carriage cover shielding a baby from the sun. Make out seats. They had a great jukebox as well, playing rhythm and blues to the Great American Songbook, to Edith Piaf, Mel Tormé, Ellington, to Broadway show tunes, to cuts from student productions like the Hasty Pudding show. I met Olivia at the Casa B, hanging out with friends of mine.

Olivia was at Harvard Law School, one of the very few women there in the 1960s. We ended up that night singing along with the jukebox, show tunes, karaoke before it was invented; and we started dating. The first James Bond novels were just becoming popular and I was hooked on them. One night I was picking Olivia up at her dorm, excited to see her, the first rush of romance, so much unknown, one of the best things in life, the discovery phase.

I was on time but I waited for her for half an hour, watching the other guys waiting also, Saturday night rituals, their dates coming down from their rooms, "Sorry, sorry. Hairdryer broke. My folks called. Studying, forgot time." They'd all be happily, shyly, nervous, then out into the night. Olivia smiled her way into the reception area. "Sorry, sorry. But it'll be worth it."

It seems parking a car in those days was never a problem. I had a Volkswagen Bug and paid no attention to legal or illegal spaces, just stick it in somewhere and be an optimist. I unlocked the Bug and immediately saw a wrapped package on the driver's seat. "How the hell did this get here?"

"The fairies probably left it," Olivia said, completely unsurprised.

"The car was *locked*."

"Open it."

Inside the package was a black wool knit sweater, like a varsity sweater. On the front, a knitted red "007" in block numbers. Olivia was smiling a secret little smile like a Bond heroine. "Live up to it," she said.

She was late meeting me because it took her a little longer than she thought to jimmy open my door. She had knitted the sweater herself; one of the best presents I ever received.

I can't say she loved me. But she believed in kindness and, as she told me, "Always be a surprise to people, and never really show 'em your hole card; keep a little in reserve for yourself." I've taken this to heart, realizing that no man I've ever met would give me this advice. And in a 007 sense, Olivia would have been an excellent spy.

At one point that fall, we both had reasons to go to Manhattan. "Let's take the train," she said.

"Bus is cheaper."

"Nope. The train. Trains are romantic. In four hours, a train trip is the single best way to find out if there's really something in the relationship. You're locked up with each other and no one can get away." On the journey she taught me the hand signals that traders used to transmit orders on the old American Stock Exchange, which started outdoors originally with men signaling with hand movements to buy and sell stocks. The Exchange was nicknamed "The Curb," because when it was founded, the members operated out of doors, literally on the curb. And I told her about the wild characters I'd met during my own Wall Street training program.

When we got to Grand Central, she hugged me and said, "Well, it's workin' so far." I guess we both passed the train test. I still use this in relationships and the best compliment I can give anyone is, "You're never boring."

> IF YOU WANT TO REALLY TEST A RELATIONSHIP, TAKE A FOUR-HOUR TRAIN TRIP, NO DEVICES, JUST TWO PEOPLE SEEING IF THEY CAN MAKE THE TRIP WITHOUT BORING EACH OTHER.

8 | SEDUCTION

We men can learn a lot from women who are *not* uplifting, who can be dangerous as well.

One of my very best friends in college was a fool for marriage; he could not be without a wife. He became a prominent divorce attorney, one who always wanted harmony for both the parties involved, a lover of people. He and his wonderful first wife got divorced. One reason was that he had a roving eye, and like many marriages in the 1950s, people married young, right out of college. When the birth control pill triggered the sexual revolution, he complained to me, "The world is four-and-a-half billion years old ... and I was born *five years* too soon." He also got lost on the side roads of life. While practicing law, he began taking classes at the Museum of Fine Arts, going for a graduate degree. He painted. He read Horace in the original Greek, he wrote a 1,000-page novel (unpublished), about an island where mice ruled. "Any sex in it?" my wife asked him.

"No," he answered, "sex will be in the sequel."

He paid attention to the sidebars, the asterisks, much more than the really important things: his marriage, his profession, his kids. He married a second time, to an English teacher, sharing a love for books. He assumed at the time and said to me, "This is it, talking about books for evermore with her. That's our future."

Time and another child, while bumping along with his sidebars. At that moment, a paralegal at his office began working closely with him on a number of matters. The working relationship gradually became a friendship.

Since my friend seldom paid attention to what was *really* important and loved the sidebars, the paralegal filled that slot. She had been divorced, also talked about books ... but many other things as well.

My friend liked to celebrate his birthday with trips abroad. One fall he and his wife went to England for his 55th, starting in Stratford where the birthday dinner would be held and they could lose themselves in Shakespeare, and debate whether he indeed wrote all the plays attributed to him.

As they came down the inn's main staircase to dinner, they saw a large banner hanging down from the ceiling, displaying a message anyone descending the stairs would immediately notice. The message said, "Happy Birthday to Puck." Puck, the sprite in *A Midsummer Night's Dream*.

"Oh joyful day," my friend said, delighted that his wife created this surprise. She acted as excited as he. "You don't have to order," the maître d' told them. "We pay attention to special guests."

There were escargot and Dover sole and venison with wild rice and a red currant based sauce, a small salad with walnuts and a fine Stilton. At each course my friend marveled at every bite, knowing his wife had surprised him in such wonderful ways. But at each bite's gushing, she would say, "No idea. Not me. What a travel agent." Every course involved his favorite dishes. "Soup to nuts," he said.

Dessert time, the lights were lowered and, from the kitchen, in marched the pastry chef, wearing an immaculate white toque, and accompanied by the rest of the kitchen staff. They marched to my friend's table, the pastry chef carrying a Grand Marnier soufflé, also my friend's favorite.

As the chef presented it to my friend and his wife, the chef with a flourish, bowed and removed the toque. It was my friend's paralegal, who, knowing their itinerary, created the entire evening, sold the inn a bill of goods and carried it off.

When my friend told me the story upon his return, he looked at me with a little smile and said, "I didn't realize how unhappy I was in my marriage."

The paralegal became wife number three. They were married for several years, until she maneuvered him into moving from the country to a prime space in the city. The week they moved in, she announced that *she* wanted a divorce. She got the house she had cherry-picked. My friend moved on to find wife number *four*.

This story underscored for me this lesson:

IF YOU'RE MARRIED, YOU'D BETTER PAY
ATTENTION EVERY DAY TO WHETHER YOUR
SPOUSE IS HAPPY OR NOT.

9 | MAKING YOUR CASE: MARRIAGE

No one really can give you advice about marriage before you're actually in the experience. Most of my friends in college married whoever they were dating at the end of senior year. They were all children really, knowing only that they were probably in love. But, on-the-job training is probably the best education. I married later than most of my friends, selfishly because I wanted a writing career, and until it was launched I didn't want to have a partner. "If I cannot make myself happy," I used to tell people, "I can't make anyone else happy." When I had a contract for my first novel I was 28 years old. I married the next year.

We rented an apartment in the city for a few years. Then the time came when we could afford to buy a house, and I wanted to stay in the city. My wife wanted the country: a lawn, trees, privacy. We went back and forth on this until she said to me, "Do we laugh together?"

"Yes."

"Do you respect strong opinions?"

"Yes."

"Well, how about this for the next 50 years? When we're stuck on a subject that we both care about, the person who wins the argument is the person who is *really* passionate. Who wants it so much more than the other person. I *really* want to live in the country, see the seasons change in the trees and the flowers."

I thought about this for a while and said, "As you're talking, I'm imagining a house. I never believed I could afford a house. But promise me this can work in *my* direction too."

"Promise," she said. We moved into a 100-year-old yellow clapboard farmhouse.

Some years later when our middle son was nine, I wanted him to go to a Jewish boys' summer camp where I had been a counselor. Susan thought it was a terrible idea. It had been a magical place for me, mostly because the owner taught the absurdity of life and educated little boys in the comedy in movies and television, and musical comedy in theater. His counselors taught athletics and crafts and caring about others. They were hired partially for their sense of humor. Susan agreed that I cared much more than she did about this, and off he went, eventually becoming a counselor as well, and making his living as a director of comedy commercials.

Susan was responsible for shaping my views about compromise. It worked for us for forty-six years.

MAKE YOUR CASE:
THE MOST PASSIONATE PARTNER WINS.

10 | THE SHORTSELLER

Amy Wilson walked into my office years ago on an errand of mercy. She was vetting money managers for a friend from Israel and she had heard about our group from several friends. "I wanted to make sure no one would take him to the cleaners," which made me immediately like her. My partners and I told our story, and she left with her Israeli friend, thanking us for our time. He came back to us. So did Amy.

Every day when I get up, I hope to learn something valuable or interesting from the people who cross my bow.

Amy is a partner in a hedge fund. Her specialty is "selling short," betting that she and her investors can profit when stocks go down. As we got to know each other I asked her, "Don't you know that it's supposed to be un-American to bet that things will fail? This is the land of opportunity."

I was kidding. Amy said, "Ahhh, but opportunity can cut *both* ways." As I've said, almost all of my best friends, women and men, are what I call "bent," people who always felt they were loners and different, no matter how social they might appear. These friends tend to be original thinkers, and no matter what organizations they belong to, they tend to be observers, outsiders looking in, noses pressed to the glass.

Amy grew up in Pennsylvania and majored in economics and East Asian studies at Penn State.

My great Aunt Marsha had also told me when I was a little boy, "Never ask boring questions." Because of her, I always ask people about their early lives, what formed them. People love to talk about themselves once they get the sense that you're actually interested in them.

"I had a language requirement," Amy told me. "I hated French," she said. "So I did, in my own way, research and thought I'd go with the future, meaning the Far East, billions of people. I narrowed it down to China and Japan, ultimately studying Chinese."

"Why?" I asked. She smiled. "Because if I moved to Japan, I thought, there's no real future for women in Japan, because of how the society was structured. But ... different in China. So I took Mandarin and then went to Taiwan for a semester abroad."

Again, because of Aunt Marsha, one of the things I ask people about is high school, sometime in everyone's life that is/was transformative, for better or worse. Ask anyone, "What were you like in high school?" and almost everyone will answer ... "Oh, God." But it's a good starting point for relationships.

"Studying Chinese took me into a different world," Amy said, "something out there beyond Pennsylvania. To underscore this, I played Carrie Pipperidge in our school's production of *Carousel*, you know, 'When I Marry Mr. Snow.' I had a lousy voice, but it also took me into a world beyond where I lived."

Amy won a Harry S. Truman Scholarship doing that semester abroad in Taiwan and went on to Harvard Business School.

"I loved the intellectual side there; not so much the personal. You can't believe how happy I was to talk business all day. I was in a section with about 80 people. Twice they gave me 'The Shark' award. The first time I got it, I cried. But later I took it as a badge of honor. And I realized that what I wanted to do with my life was to 'find something that no one else has figured out.'"

After college, Amy did various things to find her calling. She interned at Corning in upstate New York. She worked at Merck, the pharma giant, as a drug rep. "My territory in New York City was between 62nd and 80th Street, and our quota was to see seven doctors a day, whether we worked in Ames, Iowa, Austin, Texas, or Manhattan. I could do my job in three hours a day, driving around in my Dodge Dynasty. Eighty percent of our sales reps were young women. Why? Because you broke up their monotony of seeing patients all day. The drug companies did their homework, a good rep could make a lot of money, and it taught so much about the psychological side of business.

"One of the jobs I sought at the time was at the NSA, the National Security Agency. After months of interviews, they offered me a job. But I asked almost everyone I met at Fort Meade where they interviewed me and gave me lie detector tests, 'Are you happy in your job?' Virtually everyone I asked said '*no*.' So I turned them down."

For the last five years she has been a partner in a Boston hedge fund, "doing deep dives on what can go *wrong* with a company."

"Whatever prompted you to make a living betting against things?"

She thought a bit and said, "I think it comes from childhood, when my mother kept telling me that when I grew up I should be either a nurse or a librarian. Because 'when bad times came, you'll always have a job.' I think that was burned into my brain."

People's brains do absorb lessons from childhood that others preach. Smart people often reject, as they grow, those lessons that don't seem to apply to them.

"People used to tell me in high school, 'Behave like everyone else.'

Well, I couldn't do it and I still can't. But you do learn to adapt to the notion of what can go wrong," she says.

"I did get divorced after having two children, my girls. And you never really know anything until you *live* through it.

"I fired my first divorce lawyer. She had the annoying habit of calling me when she was driving to the Cape on weekends. I felt she was using me as an ATM, making sure she got paid on her way to her pleasure. She also urged me to settle my divorce. I fired that lawyer and told her, 'I believe in equality. But not when I'm getting divorced.'"

I've asked Amy about her methods in selling stocks short. Here's one example of her technique: "ADT, the home security company," she had told me, "I sold it short in April 2013, at $48. Bulls (people who believed in it), did not recognize that Comcast was launching its own security solution at a loss to keep cable customers. Comcast was installing very elaborate systems in customers' homes and charging low monthly fees if customers would extend their cable contracts. To compete, ADT was forced to install similarly elaborate systems (e.g., with surveillance cameras), with low monthly fees. I had Comcast and ADT salespeople come to my home to verify my thesis. ADT's numbers supported the thesis, with its customer acquisition costs ballooning and its attrition rates rising. In addition, I spoke to regional security companies who explained that once the initial ADT contract ended, the regionals would take over the account for a lower monthly fee, using the equipment already installed by ADT.

"I closed the position at $31.40 on January 30, 2014."

This means that Amy made a profit for her clients (the difference between $48 and $31.40; about a 17-point gain). If the client had 1,000 shares, they made $17,000 (short term), before taxes.

———

It's the process I love. Amy had Comcast and ADT come to her *home*. Women on a regular basis make me say, "I would never have thought of that." I would find it a lot safer in our society if she *had* joined the National Security Agency.

> ALWAYS CONSIDER WHAT CAN GO WRONG IN ANY PLAN NOT JUST WHAT CAN GO RIGHT.

11 | THE TOUGH STUFF

Street-smarts trump genius every time, in my opinion, particularly in our everyday lives. Not the genius to cure cancer or heart disease, but in the daily struggles to stay calm and sane, the down and dirty practicality of life. In my office, for the last 30 years, Lee Tibbetts has made the business run smoothly, doing what she does best, "cutting through the fog," as she says.

Lee grew up in the strict Catholic environment of South Boston, the mainly Irish neighborhood you've seen in movies like *Mystic River* and *The Departed* and *Good Will Hunting*. I've often said that to understand Boston you have to know our city is all about three things: sports, politics ... and revenge. The revenge part came mostly from growing up in blue collar or immigrant neighborhoods where generations of families lived. People often carried grudges and enmities from childhood. In telling stories of growing up this way, you often hear the phrase, "We never knew we were poor." Because the neighborhoods knew commonality, they made up their own fun and games, with no parental supervision. Lee grew up with three sisters, and everyone took care of each other. "How Catholic were we?" She answered her own question. "Well, for instance, on Holy Thursday, before Easter, my father would take us to seven churches. My parents wanted to name me Lee Marie, and Dad went to our parish priest and asked him if they could name me that. The priest opened a window in his office and yelled out to the street, 'Lee Marie! Lee Marie … ' He looked at my dad. 'God says it's a fine name.'" The same priest would not give them permission to go to a friend's Protestant wedding. "It's a sin," the priest told them.

When Lee married, her husband was in the Navy, stationed in San Diego. "I had to work too. I got a job selling men's shoes. The salesmen resented me. 'Hey,' I told them, 'When *I* buy shoes it's a guy who always fits me. What the hell does a guy know about fitting women? As far as I can tell, all you care about is looking up their legs.' I had learned by then not to be the quiet little Catholic girl who never went to college, but learned typing in high school, that if you stood with your head down in the back of the room, you'd probably stay there for the rest of your life.

"But in San Diego, one weekend, my husband took his Harley out for a ride and got into a horrendous accident. He was in a coma and was not expected to make it." Lee was 29 with two little children, 7 and 10. Her husband stayed in a coma for months. He came out of it, paralyzed. Lee's three sisters, were all of modest means, in a time when long-distance phone calls, particularly cross-country, were expensive. They set up phone chains. Someone called her every day. Right after the accident, they pooled funds, flew to San Diego to rally around Lee. "The family was tight, *is tight*. Our strong faith helped as well. But my sisters, so strong, poured their strength into me and made me believe there was nothing we could not do pulling together." They moved to Boston and a brother in law, who worked for Lehman Brothers, got Lee a job in the financial world at a time, the early '80s, when women were mostly secretaries or the occasional back office worker.

"The office manager," she told me, "was a great guy, loosey-goosey but smart; knew how to protect his turf and was good to his people. He put me in charge of operations, like a supply chief in the Navy. I told the manager, 'I've never done any of this before.' He told me, 'The worst thing that could happen to you already happened. Think about it. Create your space … on the job training.'"

Lee had to order supplies, deal with vendors, make sure the technology worked, heard requests and complaints from the brokers, opened the office in the morning, closed it at night. "I knew nothing about nothing," she told me. "I cried every day and every night … I'd go up on ladders to snake electrical wires through the ceiling tiles, tape 'em to the corners of walls, I'd stay 'til midnight, work weekends when new brokers came in. I'd get them desks and chairs, make sure computers functioned; teach 'em the ropes."

Lee talks fast, no nonsense, gets to the point.

"Everybody was a guy then, no women brokers and ten percent of that male population was a pain in the ass, demanding. *Why is a woman telling me what to do?* Asshole behavior. I realized I had made it when I came in one morning, picked up my coffee mug. Someone had written in magic marker, the C word on the cup. I know I burst into tears, going to a ladies room stall so no one could see me. Then I thought, 'I'm stronger than that prick … and I'm good at my job.' I showed the cup to the manager and he basically laughed. I loved the guy in many ways. But he *laughed*. 'They're never going to beat me,' I said to myself.

And they haven't."

Lee's grandson, Daniel, now works for our group as a sales assistant, keeping with our description of our team (by one of the partners), as the "Island of Misfit Toys." Daniel works both sides of his brain. In his case, the music business would be his first love. Breaking into the music business, in my view, is even tougher than making a dent into movies. But gaining an education into markets and wealth management can provide a base for almost anything you may want to pursue. He has told me, "My grandmother has not been shy in teaching me lessons all of my life. One story about her sticks in my memory, though, because I was a little boy at the time and nervous about the older boys in school. She always rode the subway in and out of work. One day she was coming home and the car was packed. An older Asian man was seated near her, looking down, minding his own business. Four teenage boys stood in front of him, taunting him, poking him in the chest with their fingers. My grandmother told me, 'Everyone around us looked away, pretending it wasn't happening, covering their faces with newspapers they were reading. I said, loud and clear, so everyone could hear, "Hey leave the guy alone. What would your mother say if she caught you acting like this? What would you do if a pack of hooligans did this to your mothers?" People started to clap. The boys got off at the next stop. One of them gave me the finger. But his buddies pulled him off down the platform. Even punks,' my grandma said, 'if they care about *one* thing … it's their mother. You want to shame any guy, use the *mother* word.'"

I asked Lee about the story. "Yeah," she said, "little boys are scared of anyone who doesn't look like them. My deal is that, if you've had a paralyzed husband for many years, and you had to pull the wagon by yourself, telling a few pissant boys about life is nothing. *Nada*."

IF YOU KNOW YOU'RE RIGHT, DON'T TAKE
ANY GUFF FROM ANYONE.

12 | CURIOUS GEORGE

Margret Rey helped create the monkey Curious George with her husband Hans. He did the delightful drawings. I met Margret after Hans had died. We shared an editor at my then publishing house and he referred her to me. "She needs a lot of help with her money," he said, "and it keeps pouring in. But I have to say she can be a bit unusual ... difficult in fact. So I don't know whether I'm doing you a favor or not."

"Let's give it a whirl," I said.

Mrs. Rey arrived for her first appointment walking in as if she were Catherine the Great, taking the measure of an opposing general. She was naturally suspicious.

I work on the 39th floor of a high-rise in the midst of Boston's financial district. My view looks out upon Boston Harbor in one direction and over the Charles River as it bends towards Cambridge and Fenway Park in the distance.

"Isn't this a great view?" I asked her, "out to the harbor and the other side follows the Charles River."

She scowled at me. "Never mind about the view," she snapped in a strong German accent. "Just make me some money."

Margret Rey was the toughest person I've ever dealt with in business. She punished people for what she saw as inefficiency and stupidity. She was smart and she understood early that the endless people and organizations who wanted her money as contributions would have to pay the price in emotional tribute to her. She could be harsh. A neighbor of Margret's told me this story. "We lived across the street from the Reys. One week we were having the outside of our house painted, a traditional revolutionary Cambridge house yellow. Margret came out to watch the job and I came over to say hello.

"'What are you doing?' Margret asked me.

"'We are painting our house,' I replied. 'It's the same color as all of those Brattle Street houses.'

"Margret looked at me, a hooded look.

"'But those are *beeyooutiful houses*,' she replied. Then she turned on her heels and walked away."

Money always draws a crowd. It took several years for Margret Rey to even partially trust me, and she never did completely. Part of the reason was that she and her husband Hans, the artist and creator of the monkey, pedaled across France and Spain, Curious George drawings rolled into their simple suitcases, to escape the Nazis. She felt that she had to be really tough to survive. But she continued to brutalize people. One night I took her to dinner at a small neighborhood Cambridge restaurant near her house. As we walked in, we passed the great satirical songwriter, Tom Lehrer, whom I knew.

"Hi Tom," I said. I resisted the urge to be clever with him, since it would have been fruitless with a legend. So I introduced Margret to him and his companion. Margret paused a beat, leaned down to Tom Lehrer, and said, "You used to do something. Why don't you do it anymore?" She didn't care. Unspeakable things had happened to people she knew. Being demanding of others didn't bother her at all.

Margret would never specifically give me advice. We lived on separate islands, paddling around each other. But observing her I learned a lot, about survival, about when to draw lines in the sand regarding other people's behavior, about earning trust. One day she called me and said, "What is the Danish krone?" Thinking quickly, I realized that she had probably gotten a royalty check in Danish currency and wanted to know what it translated to in US dollars.

"Margret," I said, "I've got to call a money desk at a bank and get the current conversion." She contemptuously said into the phone, "Don't you know *anything?*"

Slam. Disconnect.

Here's the first lesson I learned from Margret Rey: She will punish you till the cows come home unless you push back. Her technique of intimidation was amazing to watch and hear about. She was famous in Cambridge for walking into the neighborhood post office, seeing only one clerk in place out of four stations and exclaiming in a booming voice, "Is no one working here? We are taxpayers and you're cheating us out of our money. Get back to work!" One day, exasperated in a phone call to her I said, "Look Margret, I admire your tough-mindedness, but you really need me in your life. Money is not my God and I don't have to pick your pockets to support my family. I treat you with respect. How about getting the same from you?" Silence on the other end, then a hang up. But from then on a nice detente. Her behavior again taught me that if you did not confront bullies head-on you would continue to be abused.

If you work in the securities industry you have to put up with enormous layers of bureaucracy, endless government regulations and scrutiny of almost all of what they consider "outside activities." This includes communicating to the public in writing. Originally these rules were put in for good reason: to prevent people in finance from making outlandish promises of riches and profits. "Buy Raging Porcupine mines, it's going to triple," for instance. The rules were not put in for writers of novels, or for professional literary people.

I have been a member of the Author's Guild since 1967, and earned money from this other life for every year since then. This other life in many ways, fuels my life in the stock markets, understanding human nature, fear and greed as tools to analysis. But with every book, I'd had to go through the drill with firm lawyers. "Why are you writing this? Why should we give you permission? What purpose does this serve?" Sound like the Inquisition to you? Years ago, after I had known Margret for some time and absorbed her unusual way of dealing with people, I was questioned again, on a conference call with several lawyers in my firm. Most people in this situation generally feel as if they are guilty of something, some heinous crime. They feel on the spot, like rogue cops being questioned by Internal Affairs. Channeling Margret and surprising the interrogators, I went on the attack. The call lasted about 18 minutes, and I spoke for 16 of them, detailing my writing history, telling them it was obvious they had never read a memo about this I had sent down a month before. When I was done with my rant ... silence from the other end. Then, "Would you send us a copy of the book for our review?"

"I put body and soul into my writing," I said. "I work too hard on my books to give them away, if you want to read it and you might benefit from it, it should be in every bookstore, on Amazon, on e-books, and audio. I'm not sending any freebies."

That was the end of the conference call. And I got approval from the firm the next day. My manager got an email from the chief lawyer: "That was the most amusing conference call I've had in 22 years in the business."

Thank you, Margret Rey.

I had urged Margret to start a foundation, since so much money flowed from the monkey's adventures. She resisted this idea until pushed over the edge by young woman from Malaysia, Lay Lee Ong, who had rented rooms in the Rey house while she was a graduate student. Lay Lee became a surrogate daughter to Margret. "I'm going to toughen her up," Rey told me, "teach her about the realities of life." Lay Lee Ong is both smart and funny, an unbeatable combination. She became Margret Rey's friend and confidant, and Lay Lee convinced her to establish the Curious George Foundation. She and Margret were the trustees, along with me, the caboose, speaking when spoken to.

After Margret's death a big problem appeared for the estate. Lay Lee told me that on Margret's deathbed she had said, "I regret that I never did enough for the Jews." I never really knew about Margret's ethnicity, she was a force unto herself.

It turned out one of her grandfathers had been the Grand Rabbi of Hamburg.

Margret's estate was divided between a small number of nonprofit organizations, almost all with a green, quite liberal orientation; her preference for philanthropy. Lay Lee, a better daughter to her mentor than any real daughter probably would have been, had been left a seven-figure trust account, one that would have provided for her nicely for the rest of her life. But she honored the memory of Margret and she disclaimed any interest in the trust account, deciding to give it entirely to Combined Jewish Philanthropies in honor of Margret Rey's German parents in a donor advised fund. I know many generous, philanthropic people. But I've never met anyone in my life who has given up total financial freedom to create a memorial for someone special in the donor's life. I call her Saint Lay Lee, and she bristles at the suggestion.

"I'll be fine," she said to me. "There is more to life than money." Saint Lay Lee Ong.

But nothing is easy. Once this piece of the Rey estate was targeted in a new direction, one of the prime nonprofit beneficiaries learned of it and their lawyers basically said, "Whoa, if you're disclaiming what you've been awarded, you've given it up and this money has to be apportioned only to the original nonprofit beneficiaries. *Not* to some glorified maid." Those were the actual words. They wanted to wipe out Margret Rey's deathbed statement, which no one but Lay Lee heard, and scoop the millions for themselves.

I knew the CEO of the imperious nonprofit institution and invited him into my office to chat about it. He was arrogant and firm, "It's ours by law."

"Did you ever think," I asked him, "of the political uproar in the community when this goes public?"

He looked at me as if to say, "How naïve can you be?" and said, "We've had bad publicity before and we'll have it again." Then he left.

I waited about two minutes and made one phone call. It was to the leading cultural columnist at the *Boston Globe*, a man who deeply despised hypocrisy, excess attitude and elitism, and wasn't afraid to make noise about it. Instead of his usual column running down the side of the page, the piece about Curious George's estate was splashed across the front of the arts section, above the fold. It got everyone's attention in this matter, the good and the bad and the ugly. It took a while longer, but the protest was dropped; somehow sanity and bad publicity tipped the scales. The Jewish charities received the funds and it has become the gift that keeps on giving, having dispensed millions of dollars to wonderful causes that would've been blessed by Margret Rey and the curious monkey.

My initial response to being bullied like this was certainly nudged along by the lessons taught me while observing Margret in action. I'm not going to shout out in post offices that everyone should return to their jobs. But after knowing her I became less hesitant to speak my mind in more forceful ways in business and social settings, and to be less tolerant when it became obvious that people weren't pulling their own weight. It's amazing how much a bit of vinegar in life can produce results. Margret could always tell when people were faking it, and she called them on it in dramatic ways. She didn't care what she said or what others thought of her. She would steamroll over you, if you let her.

ALWAYS PUSH BACK AGAINST BULLIES.
THEY WILL CAVE IN.

13 | LONELINESS

essons from women come to me from all over the place, if you're open to wisdom. My friend Joe may have had one sweetheart in his life. He dated Susan in high school, married her when he was 22 and she, 20. They were together for more than 40 years, until Sue was stricken with a virulent cancer. She died of it in weeks, leaving Joe without her for the first time since he was a teenager.

He is private to an extreme. Joe is Catholic, strong and observant in his faith. He is a friend from my summer place. He and Sue were our golf partners for many years, forging our bonds with contests, that were not contests as much as walking and shooting the breeze about life. When both our wives died, my daughter became my golf partner. Joe invited several women friends to join in our course therapy, and we plowed on. But none of these women were romantic interests. None of them eased his pain.

But this summer he introduced us to a woman who he met at a dinner party last fall in our community. Tabby is a businesswoman, a pro at her job. She was from Chicago and has the Midwestern approach to meeting new people. She welcomes them in, gives them a hug and a smile, and assumes that everyone she meets will treat her with curiosity and honest enthusiasm, which she offers back in large dollops.

Many people tend to see only today, don't really notice the world around them, worry about kids, money, retirement. They don't really plan about, "If I do X, what are the implications? What's my backup plan? How to deal with the what-ifs?" Tabby seems to think about things, anticipating the sunny side of life, "that there will someday be someone to hold me, to share what I have to give and give back to me as well."

She has lost two husbands but she packs her bags and goes on the road to work and smiles at strangers; Midwestern trust in others.

She had a double major in college, chemistry and biology, and hoped to work at Woods Hole Oceanographic Laboratories. But she was offered a job at Goodyear Rubber, selling products for their chemical division. "A chemistry major can learn how to sell," she told me, "a lot easier than a salesperson can learn chemistry."

Tabby has always been a road warrior, traveling some years over 100,000 miles, and producing at high levels for the companies she represented, a favorite of the CEOs everywhere she's been.

She can't explain why, but I think it's two main things: She's competent, believes in her products and can explain what they can do to enhance profits in simple, storytelling ways. She's kind to people, totally nonaggressive. Quiet excellence is what she projects. Early in her career at Goodyear, there was a group event to build team esprit, an outing at a park that included games like volleyball. "My boss then was on the other side of the net from me and, running to get a serve, he fell on his shoulder and couldn't lift his arm. 'I'm fine,' he said, getting up. But he obviously wasn't and everyone else felt it was not their job to question his statement of 'I'm fine.'" Tabby insisted that he go to an emergency room and she would drive him, which she did. He had a separated shoulder and needed an operation.

She left Goodyear not long afterwards. But years later, on a new job, her old boss became her boss again. He helped her up the ladder there and became her mentor and biggest supporter. "It was natural for me," she said, "to help him out. I would have done it for anyone. How could I have known that it would resonate later? But it taught me that if you show acts of kindness in a genuine way, and go 110%, that the by-product can help you in any job that you pursue. I'm a nurturer. Women are nurturers."

Seems to me that men would be well served to pay more attention to nurturing.

Here's what she taught me, a big lesson for men who are alone: bachelors, widowers, the lonely. I am often all three of those things in my free-range-chicken life.

All of the times in her adult life, when Tabby was living alone, without a husband or companion, she told me, "I always believed in hope. So wherever I lived, house or apartment, I was determined to make sure that I lived as if I was married, that someone was sharing my space, and that I cared for them. So I wouldn't be sloppy. If I were a man, with all this in mind, and I was alone, I wouldn't drink from the milk carton. I wouldn't spoon out ice cream from the container, I'd scoop it out into a proper bowl. I'd put the seat down after I'd pee. I'd assume that someday I *might* be living with someone. I might be married again. I didn't want to resent the fact that I *wanted* to drink milk out of the container. I live as if I were married so that it would be a natural segue someday to that life."

No man would have told me this. I make my bed every day. I plump the cushions on the couches. I recycle and don't cheat on it.

And I (almost) always put down the seat so that it becomes automatic.

LIVE AS IF YOU WILL SOMEDAY BE SHARING YOUR SPACE WITH SOMEONE ELSE.

14 | YOU CAN'T GO OUT LIKE THAT!

I was taking a friend to dinner at a neighborhood bistro. It was summertime and hot. He was wearing crisp Bermuda shorts, with a new striped polo shirt and a red puffy lightweight vest. "Wow," I said. "Does GQ know about you? Did you find me on Tinder or something?" He was younger than me, and a client. The bistro was a popular place and tough to get reservations there unless you were a regular. Which I was. My friend knew that the bistro was kind of a club, and that people in business, entertainment, sports, table hopped and pressed the flesh.

He blushed a quickie blush and said, "It's summer. I figured, 'just toss on my jeans and a tee shirt and head out.' My wife said to me, 'You can't go out like that. You may meet someone who counts, someone who can get you a better job. There's stains on your shirt; you've got a rip in your jeans. You look like a slob.'"

At dinner, three different people, table hopping, said to him, "nice vest." I was able to leverage that and tell them about his job search, and we got three business cards.

Only a woman would check the man leaving the house for lint, cowlicks, wrinkled jeans, stains of all kinds, and the sense that you might meet someone to take you to the next level. It wouldn't occur to most men that anyone would care about checking for stains on clothing. My wife would tell people about me, "I'm his preener ... watching out for schmutz; dusting him off, making him presentable."

I'm not proud. I ask my crew in the office every day to check me out, spinning around for their scrutiny. "It takes a village," one of them said to me. But it makes me feel better about myself.

You're lucky if you have a woman to spot your flaws.

IMPORTANT OUTINGS: HAVE A WOMAN
CHECK YOU OUT FIRST.

15 | THE MONEY GAME: FINDING YOUR NICHE

My friend Kathleen loved the financial markets years ago and believed she could become an effective stockbroker, now called "wealth managers." Even 25 years ago, women stock brokers, or financial consultants, were rare in the industry. We did not take trainees in our office, but our firm had another office in the city that trained new brokers. I pleaded Kathleen's case to our regional manager, telling him how effective she had been running several small businesses of her own, and how the future should probably be much brighter for women in finance. The regional manager thought it would be a good idea and arranged an interview for her at another office we owned in our city. She interviewed with "Fat Tommy," what we called the office manager who used to pass out beer to his troops every day when they passed certain benchmarks in commissions. They even carried beer illegally in the Coke machines.

It was often "party time" at Fat Tommy's office. She called me after her interview.

"What did Fat Tommy say?" I asked her.

"I heard him on the phone as I waited outside his office," she said. "He was talking to some honcho in New York, and he said, 'If Spooner thinks he's gonna shove some broad down my throat, he's got another thing coming.'"

He didn't hire her. But I pushed and she did get into one of our suburban offices, where within eight months she became the biggest producer of business in that office. I used to mail Fat Tommy proof of her accomplishments. He never answered any of them but I got an enemy for life, and happy to have him for an enemy.

When Kathy started in the investment business, she chose her clothes each day as if she were going into battle: choosing suits of armor, power suits. For three years, she battled to find her niche; her specialty where she could separate herself from the crowd. After a few years of this struggle, on a gutsy move, she went on trips to the Far East, on her own dime, hoping to interest Hong Kong and Taiwanese businessmen to invest in America's markets. She was heavy on the gold jewelry then, and the diamonds, and the South Sea pearls. Kathy figured the richer she looked, the greedier she would make the Chinese gentlemen. One Taiwanese man who owned shoe factories asked her a long question in Mandarin. An interpreter listened and said to Kathy, "Mr. Wu admires your jewelry. He wants to know if you received these as presents or bought them for yourself due to your success in managing money."

"Tell him I bought the jewelry myself," she said. The interpreter translated, and Mr. Wu smiled. Kathy did not get the business and later asked a host about it.

"Ahhhhh," said the host, "Mr. Wu thinks that a really smart person would be able to get such glorious jewelry as gifts from others and invest her own money that she made."

"But he asked such an impolite question," Kathy said. "I know that the Taiwanese are much more subtle than that." Her host nodded. "It's probably because Mr. Wu was educated in the United States and got into bad habits. He went to Yale."

After Taiwan, Kathy threw herself into products strictly recommended by her firm, products that mostly crashed and burned. Then she had a brief foray into options, then bonds, then international mutual funds. Through all these metamorphoses, Kathy never felt that she was in control, never felt that she had found her specialty. One day, after walking through a picket line the Teamsters had set up in Chicago outside the restaurant that was the model for "cheeseburger, cheeseburger," she had an epiphany.

"*Unions,*" Kathy thought. "I'll pitch the unions."

Through some family connections, Kathy had a strong entrée into several public employee and local teachers' unions. By this time, she had determined that she couldn't run money herself. She was a marketer. She could bring the clients in, then she would farm the management of the monies out to assorted professional management firms in various disciplines (international, emerging growth, large blue chip, etc.). The fees the investor (the unions), would pay, would be split between Kathy's firm, the investment advisors ... and Kathy. She would be the quarterback, allocating the union funds between various managers. With other people actually managing the money, ideally, she would be free to go out marketing to new clients. She would never have to be in the office and the fees would come rolling in, good markets and bad ... evergreen. But money always draws a crowd, and union pension funds can contain tens, if not hundreds of millions of dollars in assets. So there is hot competition among investment people to pin these monies down for themselves and their firms.

Kathy has high energy and she is honest. "I was recruited to pitch a number of accounts, in competition with others," she said. "In five competitions, I was told that my presentation was brilliant, my slide show the best, my overall performance the most professional. But I finished second every time. Second out of six, five, three competitors. But second. I'm an optimist," she told me, "I always thought, 'next time, it's me.' Well," she went on, "next time it's a $50 million pension fund for the benefit of a relatively small carmen's union, you know, the guys who run trolleys and buses. I'm up against three other firms and the pitch is in some Italian restaurant on the south shore, the kind with the melted wax on the Chianti bottles and fried calamari for $3.95. Cocktail hour goes on for two hours and I'm drinking club soda with olives in an old-fashioned glass so the boys think I'm throwing back the martinis. At dinner," she went on, "I'm sitting in between two very nice guys. The man on my left talked to me about nothing except his children and my children. The man on my right only talked to me about my schools, his schools, and the decline of education in America. What unnerved me somewhat was the conversations on their part seemed almost rehearsed, both formal and forced. The only natural thing anyone said to me was said by the man on my right who told me, 'Never say no to seconds on veal parm, Kathy. You never know when you'll be in a position in life when you ain't even offered firsts.' Then he apologized."

Kathy told me that after dinner, she and two others, both men, gave their presentations for possible management of the pension plan. She was the only one with a slide show, performance projections and choices of various investment managers. During Kathy's performance, she glanced over at the president of the union. He was slumped down in his chair, his head back, his mouth wide open, snoring away.

At the end of the evening, the man on her right at dinner escorted Kathy to her car. He had finished several grappas and was wobbly in the parking lot. "You remind me of my daughter," the man said. "Uh, oh," Kathy thought, "here it comes."

"The truth's sad sometimes. You gave the best presentation by far," he said, "but you're never going to get the business."

"Why not?" She asked, her arms suddenly very tired, carrying her presentation materials.

"Because twice a year we go away for board meetings. We play golf, we drink beer, we gamble and we shoot the breeze about life, you know what I'm saying? You are never going to come in first, and that's the sad truth." After that debacle, she decided she needed to get out of the suburban office and move into the city. She interviewed a manager in the other firm's Boston office. He said to her, "What do we need with a woman from the suburbs around here?" She stayed with us and they moved her to an in-town branch.

Kathy never quit on anything in her life. So she thought back about what the union man had told her, and she thought about her career, and where her focus should be. The next week she went to a baseball game with her husband. Seated right in front of them was a whole section of nuns, drinking Cokes, eating hot dogs, cheering the hits. After the third inning, Kathy elbowed her husband. "That's it," she said.

"What is?" he asked.

"*The nuns!*" Kathy exclaimed. She was off to the races, calling on various charitable organizations and orders around the country and very successfully establishing her niche. "Where else can you do a good job for people financially and, after every phone call, get the blessings of the Virgin Mary called down upon your head as well?"

Kathy, as do almost all of my women friends, mentors younger people coming into, or thinking of coming into their professions.

Here are some of her observations that she passes on to others seeking her experience:

1. I'm old-fashioned. My Dad ingrained in us: stay together. In the summers, all my brothers and sisters (eight of them), stay in the same community and see each other constantly. I can't wait for the summers every year. When I tell friends about this, both old and new, they universally say, "How horrible." That's because, in my experience, many families cannot stand each other. In my case, they're my rock; it's what I count on, that close therapy, once a year. Most people *never* have it.

2. Because of this family orientation, I had to choose a career

carefully. I was 38 years old and had been a housewife for 18 years when I decided to get a job. Can you "have it all?" Well, I knew I probably only had a 20-year job life and probably the corporate life would be impossible. So I chose something, financial services, where I could mix house and career. Because you never know how your kids are going to grow up and what extraordinary needs they might have. As a financial consultant you essentially work for yourself, no matter whose name is on the door. As you start out in life as a young woman, pick a career that can build in a potential family life and try to make it something as comfortable as possible. But bear in mind, if you go this route, it will be the job and the family. Period. *You will be forced to sacrifice social life and even friendships.*

3. Staying connected to old friends, who you most treasure, is difficult, but you must free yourself to do it, even if it's sending birthday cards and being organized about these dates.

4. It may sound hokey, but I read some motivational books. But mostly I read with history in mind, so that I can learn about the past and not be so surprised about the complexities of human nature. The motivational stuff I read because I want *pull-ups* in life and not pull-downs. Pull-downs just sap so much energy. But it's from history that I learn how little changes in our hopes and fears.

5. When I first went to work, I believed blindly in everything I heard and in everything that management spouted. I thought I had to rely on others. This was a big mistake, when I realized that fundamentally I was smarter than so many of the so-called experts. The big lesson: You cannot rely on anyone else's opinion. What has been the biggest change in the financial industry has been how much more professional it's become. Leadership used to be the seat of the pants and the "buddy business." Those days are long gone.

6. Anything is achievable if you are willing to pay the price. This sounds so simple. But most people don't recognize this price, what it takes to become an astronaut, or an Olympian, for example. I suggest, if you are young and have ambitions and goals, that you keep a notebook and write down positives and negatives to all the important moves you might make. It won't eliminate surprises, but it can help a lot in the decision-making process.

7. Here's how I try to differentiate myself from others, from the thousands of financial consultants out there. I present myself as being my client's advocate; I'm the family physician, if you will. I provide advice beyond investments and I call this "unrelated business services."

8. What kept me going in business is the motto I developed when I realized how inept so many people in management were. It gave me faith in myself to keep going. And every time I saw examples of inefficiency and even stupidity at upper levels of organizations, I would say ... "there's hope for all of us."

Kathy's emotional realization of what she would have to sacrifice when she went into finance woke me up. No man I ever knew ever thought about this, when going to work, never thought about "trade offs in life." We just plowed ahead, wanting to prosper, have toys, vacation in the sun. Never trade offs. Only a woman could teach me to look at life through different prisms, to anticipate the real future, not just material comforts.

THINK ABOUT WHAT YOU'LL HAVE TO SACRIFICE TO ACHIEVE WHAT YOU WANT IN LIFE.

16 | LEGAL LESSONS: VIEWS FROM THE JUDGE

There is an old line in the movie business: "funny is money." The best teachers I've ever had were both amusing and smart. I remembered their lessons better than any others; their wit remained in my brain. I know I learned more memorable lessons about the law and lawyers from my friend, Suzanne. I met her years ago when she was the divorce attorney for one of my best friends. When the divorce became final, my friend gave a cocktail party to celebrate the occasion. The first thing Suzanne said to me after hello was, "Do you know the best tribute a woman ever gave to her husband?"

"No," I answered.

"The best tribute, in my view," she said, "was the present I gave him for his 40th birthday. He's a big Democrat," she went on, "and to surprise him I went to Providence, Rhode Island, and had a picture of a donkey tattooed on my left butt cheek."

"Really," I said.

She smiled. "Really. I have a picture of it." She smiled. "I got up on our little office Xerox machine bare-butted." She opened her tote bag and pulled out a sheet of paper. There was the donkey, in black ink.

"I'll never forget you," I told her.

"That's my point," she said. "Get people's attention. Particularly since there were very few women in any law schools in America when I got the ink."

Since then we've been good friends. Over the years I referred many of my clients to Suzanne for legal work, primarily divorces. She is selectively profane, often to underscore practical points. She does not suffer fools well, but unfailingly gives smart, practical advice, direct and unconventional, always effective. Unfortunately for me and her many clients, she was named a judge by the governor and ended her career on the bench of the Superior Court.

Here are some of her adventures and the advice to me about many things that all smack of her knowledge of human nature, and the often absurd behavior around us.

"You know what quality is the most difficult to find in American society today?" she asks. "I think it's common sense. Everyone is afraid to cut through the nonsense. No one wants to make the effort to simplify things. Well," she says, "I'm the grit in the oyster shell. It's my destiny. And I like simple. For instance, often divorce comes down to the fight over who gets the pink plastic cup in the bathroom."

Early on in our friendship I asked her, "Is everything a contest with you?" She looked at me is if I were an idiot. "Hey, what's the matter with you? Every day, if we're good at what we do, we go to war. Did you ever hear of the battle of the sexes? It's eternal. Thousands of years of history. Only today, it's out in the open. Not so many years ago the man of the house gets up, goes into the bathroom: clean towels, clean socks to put on, underwear, shirts, all there. He comes down to a hot breakfast already cooking and he tosses his wife the keys to the car. 'Take me to the train, honey, and take the car for service, standard lube, no big deal, you can probably wait while they do it.' He goes off to work, interesting people with him for lunch, has lots of give and take. His wife picks him up at the train. She has dinner cooking and when they get home, she tells the kids to be quiet because Daddy 'needs to unwind.' The husband was a king. What a life. Now it's all changed. Let me tell you what's wrong today: If I were a guy, I'd fight to the death not to give this up. Stripping all the crap away, that's why the fight is out in the open. The poor bastards are confused and they resent giving up the greatest deal on Earth. But they're losing." She told me all this 25 years ago.

I would not have a business life anywhere near as successful as it is, without the perspective I could only learn from women. Here are some of Suzanne's guidelines and advice on legal and life matters: all of which have helped me shape my views of behavior.

1. Even if you're a nuclear physicist, you still need human interaction.

   And remember, in that interaction the most important quality is a sense of humor. Because people are really terrified of each other.

2. We are not practical people; we believe what we see on the screen. I have handled hundreds of divorce cases and I know that marriage is something you have to work at every day, like constantly negotiating a peace treaty. American men won't believe that you cannot just marry for love.

3. Never overlook the obvious in dealing with people on any level. Tip O'Neill once asked a woman in his district if she voted for him.

   "No," the woman said to the long-time Congressman.

   "Why not?" asked the surprised O'Neill.

   "You never asked," the woman answered.

4. Talk to people you need something from as if it's *their* problem; as if they're a person also. I call an assistant to an eye doctor, for instance (eye doctors being a class of people who can only fit you in after Labor Day 2026), and tell them, "You sound like the only really intelligent person I've talked to all day. Well, thank God, because my eyeballs are falling out." Somehow you involve them by complimenting them. No one else does it and we all want to be stroked.

5. If you can tell a joke, you'll always sell more tomatoes than anyone else.

6. When I interview young women, I don't just want them to work 70 hours a week. I want them to have a life. I want to hire a social person with street smarts. I also check her for grooming; her hair has to be clean; her clothes neat, clean and pressed. Like it or not, appearances are how we judge people at first blush. All pitches to a jury, for instance, are a sales job.

7. When you pick lawyers, relate to them, don't react to them. I want to relate, to be the key, otherwise it's going to be an unsatisfactory relationship. I want answers to questions they wish I'd ask. It's stupid to say you only want a female attorney; or that you only want a male attorney. You can tell in five minutes if your potential lawyer is truly willing to listen to you and if you relate.

8. When I prepare for trial, I shut my door, forbid all phone calls, sit for two hours and think about the case, think about what's important and think about what the other lawyer is doing. Because I focus on the real issue ... I want the jury to give my client money.

9. Check rates at the start of your problem. Don't wait for your first bill. Ask what everyone in the law offices receives: paralegals, associates, partners. And find out approximately what

the feeling is about the overall cost of doing your job.

10. Find out if your lawyer is on any big case at the time you consider retaining them. Prior commitments can put you on the back burner.

11. Don't overreact. If all I want is a man to tie a slipknot, I don't have to go to bed with him.

"I had a young associate years ago, who easily got hot under the collar," she goes on. "He was very smart, and when angry, made it obvious that he was contemptuous of most other people's opinions. No one likes to be made to feel inferior or stupid. We all have enough problems with self-esteem not to have disdain heaped upon us. My young associate went over-the-top, losing his temper over certain rules and regulations that he perceived to be idiotic and 'making zero sense.' And he sounded off to several back-office employees who viewed their behavior as just doing their jobs. One of them came to me and said, 'Who the hell does he think he is?'

"I brought my young associate into my office.

"'People have long memories for abuse,' I said to him. 'You lose control over something fairly routine, it does several things. You lose credibility with your coworkers. And you plant a seed with people that you're a bully and they will find a way to punish you in the future. People who interact with you, at work, in garages, in restaurants, plumbers, carpenters … if you're arrogant with them they can screw up your life. Anger plants the wrong seeds in others.'"

Suzanne's advice applies to the people who insist on switching tables endlessly in restaurants, who change hotel rooms on a whim, and want every hint of garlic removed from the sauce. And also for people who want to sell all of their US stocks because of problems in Malta, or the fluctuation of the Chinese yuan. These are the people who react to headlines with either panic or euphoria. In this regard, Suzanne has also told me, "When you're hot under the collar, take a deep breath, step back, and say 'if I throw a hissy, how much can it damage me?' Inflating relatively small matters can hurt you."

12. My advice to men is to learn to talk of personal things and lose the eternal guy mode of "show no weakness."

13. Expect the worst from people and you'll never be disappointed.

Suzanne called one day recently to talk about the stock market. After chatting a while I asked her if she had seen the press or TV coverage about a female state senator's son arrested for giving a wild party at his mother's house while she was away on a vacation. There was liquor and drugs present and all the kids were in high school. The senator was controversial, and in the news a lot. Suzanne went on. "As a matter of fact, the newspapers called me to comment," she said. "I told them I'd give them a reaction if they printed it exactly as I stated. They said they would and I told them, 'It's got nothing to do with the Senator. Don't you know that all teenage boys are assholes?'"

Her practicality and irreverence have given me insight into the legal profession. When we met I really had no experience with lawyers, except for the person who helped me with my first house purchase. One of her main lessons to me resonates in any legal transaction I enter ... "Make sure your lawyer understands human nature, in *all* its forms. Then they can get into the heads of their opponents."

Recently I asked Suzanne, "How come you and I are such good friends? Why me?"

"Well," she answered, "you appreciated that I was different from the usual lawyers you had encountered. You laughed at my jokes. You enjoyed being with me. But most of all ... you *listened* to me. That's what men need to learn more than anything else. *Listen to us.*"

More than anything else, that's the lesson from women men need to know ...

"LISTEN TO US ..."

17 | THE FUTURE OF HEALTHCARE: PAM McNAMARA

Arthur D. Little was America's first consulting firm, founded in 1886. Pam McNamara was their first woman CEO, appointed in 2002 to try to save the company. Pam had an early passion. There was a lot of illness in her family when she was a child, and she knew that one big path for her would be to help cure the diseases that had affected her loved ones.

Pam went to Tufts and majored in engineering. Arthur D. Little hired her right out of college. She never had a graduate degree. I think she had a PhD in intensity and a Masters in discovering ways to improve the planet and help make peoples lives better. "All through college," she told me, "I worked every week for the Army Corps of Engineers, while having a double major in Engineering and International Relations." She laughs easily. I met Pam and her husband George at a summer dinner hosted by a client. As a "free-range chicken," I often dine with couples and get to watch the dynamics from my safe spot on the other side of the table. The McNamaras seemed to have a special way with each other, as if they had found a secret. Pam was wearing a pin on her dress that night. You don't often see women wear pins these days, as informality seems to rule in fashion. The pin was a silver starfish. "I never see pins anymore," I told her. "It's lovely. Is it something that comes from family?"

"Yes," she said. "It was my mother's. She used to tell me a story about a little girl on a beach. The beach was covered with starfish, thousands of them. The little girl knew that they would all die if they weren't restored to the sea. So she began to pick up starfish and scale them into the water like frisbees. A woman came over to her. 'What do you think you're doing, little girl?'

"'I'm saving them,' she said. 'One starfish at a time.'"

Pam touched the pin, as if she were patting something precious.

She went on. "I was eventually put in charge of global healthcare for ADL, as globalization was really picking up steam at the end of the 1990s. We had two distinctly different businesses in our company. Our founder was an engineer and those strong roots remained a prime focus. We had research labs, contract research was our business in the early dotcom era, 1998–99. In Cambridge, England, for instance, we had a lab that developed what today is Bluetooth technology. Arthur D. Little had all this research, IT capabilities, plus the consulting side of our business as well. Altogether it was a $500 million business with wonderful, smart people, almost 3,000 employees at our peak.

"Always remember in business," Pam told me, "you can be *too* successful. We had built a better mouse trap and people beat a path to our door. And, like a good mystery tale, we sowed our own seeds of disaster, although, of course, we never realized it at the time." Pam went on, animated about the past and certain crossroads we all face. "The board was thinking that we needed a new CEO, and we began a major search, ending up hiring a man from GE who had been a consultant for Boston Consulting Group in the past. GE then was one of the most admired companies in the world and we thought we were lucky. He brought in his own CFO and a head of HR. He wanted them to split us into two companies and bring one of them public via Lehman Brothers. 'We'll score big on an IPO,' Lehman told us giving hockey stick forecasts, a long shaft ending in the part that strikes the puck, jabbing upwards towards the sky. We had a board of great people, Nobel prize winners, the president of MIT. Everyone bought into the projections. But HR couldn't mesh the two businesses. We started bleeding in both areas, losing business to McKinsey and BCG. Consulting expanded worldwide and we had as many as 30 different stock plans for all the different units, each acting like a Scottish fiefdom. I was brought in as CEO, the first woman ever in that role, to stop the bleeding. My strength was in healthcare. With our labs, we partnered with Zeneca, the drug company, to develop tamoxifen, a major breakthrough in breast cancer treatment. To launch it, I worked one summer seven days a week to get it finished, the pivotal project my life, and it made me more determined than ever to make the future of smart medicine my life's work.

"But ADL was too broken to save. Lehman over-promised and the divisions in the company were out of control. Too many pieces. Impossible to synchronize the parts. Lessons and scars for a lifetime."

I have to tell a story here. My old firm, Shearson, acquired Lehman Brothers in the 1990s. They had a retail arm, stockbrokers as opposed to investment bankers. We often had joint meetings in sunny places with them, boondoggles. The Shearson brokers hated the Lehman guys. They were hustlers, reminiscent of the characters in *The Wolf of Wall Street*. They mostly came from an infamous Lehman office on Water Street, near Wall Street. One of their managers was famous for saying, "Just remember boys (they were all men in those days), a customer is like a garbage bag, fill 'em up … and throw 'em out." I was given stock in Lehman, and because of their culture, rotten at the top, in my view, I gave it to charity as quickly as I could, thinking that sooner or later, it would end in tears at that firm. So I wasn't surprised at Pam McNamara's impressions. Lehman stock went to zero.

"I have to make sure you understand, the juggling act women have to do daily," Pam has told me. "But I'm one of the lucky ones. I have a real partnership with George; we both do everything, not just one role." George is *far* from a househusband. He is an expert in defense matters, having been for many years at the top of the food chain at the nuclear submarine base at Newport, Rhode Island, and is often all over the world, consulting on the issues of defense and warfare.

"We cover for each other and adapt to incredibly busy lives. I'm a blender," Pam says. "With our schedules, as our kids were growing up, it was important to bring them often to my workplace, with the purpose of introducing the children to the people I worked with. I thought that if they interacted with my coworkers and really understood what I did every day, they would not resent my work and my time away from them. Because of that real life education, son Tim is a fierce protector and advocate of women's rights, a really serious activist."

Now Pam is the CEO of a healthcare startup called Health Helm. She says, "My mantra is *always have a Plan B*. This knowledge was learned the hard way at ADL. You know that most of life is gray," she went on, "if you think about it, we're mostly in the middle and very occasionally on the extremes. But we're now in a period of history where nothing around us is gray, except of course for the daily slog we all go through in our lives. We're in so many revolutions today because of the digital age. Almost every profession transformed by it, checking screens, great and small, from when we first open our eyes to when we're about to close 'em at night." Pam held up her smartphone. "*This* is the future of healthcare. You keep saying that 'all life is relationships.' Well, get ready to have a relationship to your health and well-being, with *yourself*." Pam says, "Healthcare is the tapeworm of society; it consumes almost 18% of the GDP in America, double the cost of any other country.

It's swallowing all of us. We never know where roads will lead us. I wanted to save lives from the time I was little but I never thought of medical school. I got my degree in the hard stuff, down and dirty in the actual arenas."

Here's where Pam's company, Health Helm, is focusing:

1. We have to control costs in American healthcare. My company concentrates on the consumerism of this care.
   We want to give patients a degree of control and involvement ... personal relationships *not* arm's-length. We want to be like Disney, make your health life an *experience*, where you're not passive. This means mobile health; you track yourself through an app. You'll have this app on your phone and you self report to your nurse and your doctor, tracking your own symptoms.

2. Only 14% of hospitals have the systems to have patients interact with their phones. And 75% of all millennials surveyed want to engage this way. It *is* the future of healthcare—fewer trips to doctors offices and hospitals, monitoring vital signs.

3. Amazingly, older patients, in their seventies and beyond, want technology in their lives when it comes to their health. Biggest reason? Seniors connect with their children and grandchildren on social media all the time. They're getting used to it and it becomes second nature. Connectivity will take the friction out of the patient/doctor experience and lower costs at the same time.

4. Berkshire Hathaway, JP Morgan, and Amazon were going to join hands to create their own approach to healthcare for their employees, bypassing traditional insurance methods. This is "creative disruption" that will transform the way we interact now with our doctors and our hospitals. Mobile healthcare will be universal. The trio of companies dropped their plans. The complexities and costs doomed this effort.

5. With our app we tend to get feedback instantly and you can see on your screen if your message has been read or not. It makes the interaction on the screen a personal experience, like seeing your granddaughter take her first steps. Seniors are our most compliant generation. They want to show their families that they're "hip to the modern age," as one 84-year-old told me. And Pam adds that when she first came to Arthur D. Little as a lowly researcher, one woman supervisor told her, "Don't worry about titles or degrees. If you're curious and ask unusual, smart questions of people, you can learn *anything,* and be good at it." Women were 12% of engineering students at Tufts when I was there. Now women are 51% in that major. And when ADL made me a project manager they gave me a T-shirt that said on it, "She who would be obeyed." I didn't know at the time whether it was a compliment or a snarky comment on me. Now I take it as their understanding that I cared about people. But I worked harder than anyone else."

There are some people I meet who I say about, "I'd follow her into battle." Pam McNamara is one of them. She also has a husband who can join her in any battle. Nice to know people who can have each other's back.

IF SENIORS CAN USE TECHNOLOGY TO CONNECT TO FAMILY, THEY CAN MANAGE THEIR OWN HEALTHCARE AS WELL.

18 | ACTS OF KINDNESS

I helped a young man get into a training program at our firm. When I broke into Wall Street as a rookie, there was also a training program. It was completely loosey-goosey; "on the job" as it used to be called. I was shuffled back and forth between departments; bonds, the stock trading desk, over-the-counter (now NASDAQ), research (I stapled reports and stuffed envelopes). It was pretty much left to the trainees to find their own professors among the stockbrokers and the firm's clients in the boardroom. They were happy to share their stories and secrets if you were proactive in your own behalf. Asking people questions, forcing yourself to be curious. People love to talk about themselves. The characters in the boardroom, clients and brokers, were my graduate school. Typically, all the stockbrokers were men, perhaps one woman client, sitting in the boardroom when I was training. That woman was Bella. But everyone called her, "The Queen," for "Queen of the Boardroom." She was a fast talking, irreverent widow, quick with the comeback, and loved by everyone, mostly because of her caustic wit. Her husband had been, as she said, a "garmento," slang for being in the dress manufacturing business. He made women's blouses. Bella flirted with all the guys but had no time for me. "Come see me in 20 years," she said. "I need *men* around me, not kids wet behind the ears."

Everything has changed in the boardrooms now, including the on-the-job aspects of becoming someone who manages people's money. Today the Wall Street training programs are mostly not really training with any strong "education in life" element. They are structured to get the trainees to pass various licensing exams. And until recently, to learn to cold call, "dialing for dollars," to me a useless, demeaning exercise. Josh, the young man I helped to hire, is both earnest, and a worker. He came to me originally through a client's recommendation. I see dozens of young people a year, happy to give them a leg up in understanding our business. I knew he was relentless from his résumé, which mentioned that he had rowed varsity crew in college and was still involved on a regular basis, out on the Charles River in high-end competitive rowing. No athlete on the planet works harder than rowers. They make for wonderful employees, and are often leaders in their various careers. Their training can be daily, every day in the year.

When I said I'm "happy" to talk with young people, there are times in the investment business where there is *no* time to spend on anything but the focus on your clients. Like bear markets when you have to have a game plan, and the phones light up with incoming calls like sniper fire. As I write this, now is one of those times that test peoples stomachs and minds, as stock prices are getting crushed on a regular basis. When you read this, it could be in the midst of a wonderful stock market. Every day is different.

Josh, I think is disappointed that I'm not asking him into my office for counsel and support on a regular basis.

But one day last week, as I was wandering the office, stretching my legs, I walked through the boardroom where the rookies dwell, and noticed that Janet, one of our sales assistants, was standing over Josh and pointing out various things to him on the screen of his computer. They were deeply engrossed in conversation. Janet works on another floor. I was curious about what she was showing him and went upstairs to ask her. Because seldom do the two floors mix during the working day, and these two might never meet, unless it were in the elevator. I've known Janet for a long time; she's worked in the office for almost 30 years.

"I've got an interest in Josh, the trainee," I told her. "He's an intense young man, and I'm sure you helped him."

Janet smiled. "These kids all seem to be fish out of water," she said. "We did meet on the elevator and when I told him I had worked in the business for 30 years, he just poured it out, how much he wanted to make it, how everything seem to be a foreign language to him, and how cold calling seems to be a very unproductive way to learn a trade. How could I *not* be nice?"

She went on. "When I came into finance it was a business for old Yankees. I'm middle class Irish. My dad was a janitor at a private girls' school. He had other jobs as well. He was good to everyone and it stuck with me. It was tough when I came into a man's world. But I stuck it out. My girlfriends stuck it out too. Kept our eyes open and our mouths shut. In one office where I worked, men hired a stripper to come in to surprise our manager on his birthday. The stockbrokers and the men clients stood up and cheered. Those were the bad old days." Janet raised her voice. "We women set the stage for all the next generations. We were tough, and I'll never forget the lessons, good *and* bad.

"Josh followed me off of the elevators and out into the street, followed me for blocks to the subway, full of questions, a sponge for information that he felt he wasn't getting from his training program.

"I gave him courage to seek out people I suggested he speak with. I told him stories of the past that might encourage him to push on. 'You row on rivers. Look at this job as another race you can win.'

"In my world," Janet had said to me, "I can connect dots and build bridges for others. Above all else … be kind. That's my important lesson to the young."

TAKE THE LONGEST-SERVING WOMEN IN YOUR OFFICE TO LUNCH AND SEEK THEIR WISDOM.

19 | THE REAL ESTATE MAVEN

"**I** was always an odd stick," Lillian told me. "My parents would constantly say that no one would marry me. They were wrong." Lillian is ninety-seven years old, feisty and as clear as Tiffany crystal in her thoughts.

"Why did they think you were an odd stick?"

"Because I read all the time," she said. "My mother came over in steerage on the *Lusitania* in 1914, the last ship to get out before World War I began, after living in a Liverpool rooming house for months, waiting to come to America. So many times, my mother said she wanted to kill herself because life was so hard."

"I went to an all-girls' high school," Lillian said, "Roxbury Memorial. We had to memorize poems, and say them aloud to our class. I used to say the poems to myself, walking around Franklin Park, loving the green space and what wondering why I wasn't like all the other little girls. Which is why I escaped into poetry as a refuge. Different worlds."

Lillian met her husband to be, Harry, during World War II. "I was a wallflower, too different for the boys in Roxbury. Harry and I didn't even know if we had a good time, it was awkward for both of us. But something clicked. To tell you how my weird brain worked, I also liked the funny pages in the paper, the comics. And something I saw there stuck in my mind. After our first date someone asked me, 'Do you think you'll see that guy again?' 'Yes,' I said, 'because I managed to put my earrings in his pocket.' He'd *have* to call me. I got that trick from the funny pages. And it worked. In July 1942, we got married. It turned out that Harry loved poetry too, and the partnership lasted for 57 years until he died.

"My real estate career, like so much in life," Lillian told me, "happened by accident. Because I loved to explore our Boston neighborhood, watching who's coming and going. Our neighborhood was full of two-family houses, mostly inhabited by immigrant Jewish families, all from Eastern Europe: Russia, Poland, Latvia." She and Harry would go into the local banks, asking if any houses where they held mortgages were being foreclosed.

"You gotta understand," Lillian told me, "we had no money. But I was persistent. What do you do if you have a dream and you need money? You *borrow* it. Almost everyone in those days had *one* rich relative. A cousin had an umbrella factory. I begged him, hounded him. Finally, he loaned me $50 for a deposit on a three-family house that the bank was happy to unload. I had to pay the cousin 6% interest, which was high. But I learned from that experience: if you're sure you've found a bargain, and you have a good eye for the future, it's *okay* to pay up. We paid $2,500 for the house, fixed it up a little, and sold it for $7,500 in five years. The cousin said, 'I didn't charge you enough.'

"That's family for you," Lillian said, "in a nutshell. But, you know, in those days it was a man's world, outside of the house. I couldn't take this lying down. Everybody around me assured me

I'd never get a man. So I actually think I relaxed around them and men never intimidated me. But they seemed to get a kick out of this feisty dame. They weren't used to women like me, who wanted to learn what *they* did. And wouldn't take 'no' for an answer. I think I sought refuge in being 'one of the boys.' It was a lot better than hearing from family, 'She's eating again. Puffing up. Just put her out to pasture,' they'd say."

I originally met Lillian through her daughter. I was friendly with her and her husband, who, coincidentally is a real estate developer, and she urged me to meet her mom. "You'll come away inspired," the daughter told me, "for a number of reasons. Including that she's funny." The daughter worked with her mom.

When we first met she launched into stories, including her first forays into real estate.

As she spun history to me, I stopped her at one point and said, "None of these projects, even when you started, were simple. They were *big*. You were a two-person team. Why so complex and complicated?"

"Stop," Lillian said. "Let me tell you large. There was a big Air Force base in Chicopee, Massachusetts. It was 1980, 564 units of housing. On sale for four million. We were the high bidder out of nine bidders. Ours was 50% higher than anyone else, and, of course, we got it. At that time, despair with Jimmy Carter, gas lines in America. We called the president of Bay Bank and at the time it was almost impossible to get a loan. We offered him a 20% interest rate. He grabbed it. Well, we eventually sold off every unit and paid the loan off in six months. The bank president never talked to us again. He thought we'd be paying him 20% for *years*. We go out and kick the tires. The banker sits at a desk."

I asked her about the "Me Too" movement. She said, "Hah! There was no glass ceiling for me. I lived my life in a man's world. Harry and I would give dinner parties. After dinner, I'd go sit with the men and talk about business. The other women would talk about wall-to-wall carpeting. It was so comfortable with Harry. When we first dated no one went to bed with anyone before marriage. I read articles in the magazines and newspapers. In the old *Boston American* there was an advice column. 'When is it okay to kiss?' was one of the questions. 'After five or six dates' was the answer. That was my model."

Lillian jumped around a lot in her stories. But always had perfect pitch in her memories of deals, the interest rates, the profit and loss, the names of the people who lent her money. I mentioned her moving from timeframe to timeframe. "Hey," she said, "it's the movie of my life. If you've lived a long time and seen a lot, you jump around. One story leads to another. So, I had no money once, and no man. But after marriage, at my 25th high school reunion, I showed around a diamond lavalier I had gotten for $850. It hung around my neck and was gorgeous. One of my classmates saw it and said, 'You were always such a pisher. And look at you now.' I just smiled at her and walked away."

Lillian told me, "In every building we bought, we entered the portals of Hell." She had her principles straight. "Once we found the formula we were comfortable with, through plenty of mistakes, we stuck with it." These lessons included:

1. Only buy distressed merchandise that no one else seems to want.

2. My motto for being a contrarian was "fools rush in where angels fear to tread."

3. You have to love the whole process of what you do ... soup to nuts.

4. I learned early what an advantage a woman has over men. Bankers, lawyers, contractors were totally won over by me being feisty and cheeky. They gave me deals and rates they never would've given a man. Sing out our differences from men; *vive la différence!* I made them laugh and they treated me right.

5. Fight friendly. Ease into difficult situations.

6. With marriage: never go to bed angry. Discover things you both love. We recited poetry to one another.

"I began writing poetry," Lillian said, "a great antidote to the dollars and cents of the business. Although there is a certain kind of poetry in getting a great deal and looking at the properties you own. Everyone of them a little, or big poem in a way."

She gave me a small book of her poems, written over many years. Here's a sample of what she writes, this woman of 97 years, working both sides of the brain. If you told me that E.E. Cummings had written this one, I'd agree with you.

But it was Lillian.

> *Though this cow*
> *Does not give milk*
> *The thoughts that flow*
> *Are smooth as silk*
> *A common goal*
> *Has made a bond*
> *Of many people*
> *Who are not fond*
> *Of interlopers*
> *Who tell us all*
> *"Go kiss my ass"*

"Why don't you cash in and relax? Owning real estate has so many moving parts." She looked at me as if I were nuts. "We've got a McDonald's. We've got a CVS. Every month the checks come in. I relax when the checks come in. Every week I walk by my buildings. And I talk to them. The good thing, they don't talk back."

YOU'LL HAVE A BETTER, LONGER LIFE IF YOU WORK BOTH SIDES OF THE BRAIN, CREATIVE AND PRACTICAL ... POETRY AND REAL ESTATE.

20 | LESSONS FROM BROOKLYN

I trained for the brokerage business in New York where my first firm had its headquarters. I was paid $75 a week (approximately $375 today, figuring for inflation), and lived in a cheesy residential hotel on the Upper East Side, one pitiful chipped paint room with a sink in one corner for $35 a week. One grimy window looked out on an air shaft. I took the MTA 4 train down to Wall Street each day, wondering, "What am I doing?" and "Who am I?"

It was mostly on-the-job training, bouncing from department to department, informal. I started in the research department, stapling reports, collating, and stuffing, then sealing envelopes. Wetting the envelope's glue side with a big fat sponge. Taking hundreds of these reports to the mailroom. You were supposed to get the education by yourself, speaking to people wherever you wandered. This was tough for me. Everyone seemed so busy and I had been raised in a household where I was the only child for ten years until my sister was born. "A child should be seen and not heard," was the rule of the house. My sister fought this tooth and nail. I went with the flow, quiet, reading books as a refuge.

The investment business has become boring to me in recent years; firms churning out a certain kind of robot, shoehorned into "one-size-fits-all" boxes, not much room for the maverick. When I trained in the 1960s, the business was loaded with characters out of Dickens novels. Bigger than life, entrepreneurial, shady, profane, irreverent, boisterous, loud, greedy, funny. And a young secretary was my guide through this Vanity Fair. Her name was Barbara Walsh and she proudly came from Brooklyn. She drank black Chock full o'Nuts coffee most of the day and smoked unfiltered Lucky Strikes and swore like the Irish traders on the institutional desk. She also gave noogies; little punches with the middle knuckle, to guys on the muscles of their shoulders if they made her laugh. It was her way of applauding. But it hurt.

Barbara was assigned to shepherding me between the departments where I was supposed to train, my profane guide to Wall Street.

I asked my boss Arnie about Barbara. "Wow, how come she's not running the firm?"

Arnie took a long puff on his cigar, and he smiled a small smile. You didn't get many smiles from Arnie. He was like a quartermaster in the army, a supply sergeant, a bean counter, whose job it was to spend as little as possible in everything he oversaw, which included the training program. He was the kind of employee who always covered his tail and couldn't wait to report any disloyalties, real or imagined. "The managing partner loves her," Arnie said. "but there are times she gets a little too exuberant for a secretary." I hated Arnie. In organizations of any kind, the person I dislike more than any other, is the person who "sucks up and bullies down." Arnie was that kind of guy.

Barbara told me, "Don't waste your time on the Arnies of the world. I focus on the three most important things I have to do every day. Everything else should be *wayyyy* down the list. In this firm I know the *real* people in every nook and cranny. I'll introduce you and show you the ropes, get the real people on your side." To show me those "reallies," she took me to where she grew up, St. Brendan's Parish, in Midwood, Brooklyn. Her 'hood, Coney Island Avenue, parallel to Avenue O. When Barbara grew up there, everyone believed in the Dodgers as if rooting for them was a kind of religion bred in the bone. "We play stickball on the street," she told me. "Manhole covers line every street. If you hit the rubber ball, 'pinkies' they're called, out over two 'covers,' it's a double. Almost no one ever hit a triple. But Willie Mays stopped his car in Harlem one day and someone pitched a pinkie to him and he hit it *five covers.* It made *The Post.*" Barbara showed me her neighborhood. "They're mostly two-family houses, and a typical street is an Irish family next to a Jewish family next to an Italian family. Everybody gets along and we all play outside with each other, stoop ball, box ball, and *War,* where the girls get to shine, because it's about *thinking,* not muscles."

"I'm a tomboy," she said. "But I like to dress up too. I wear my Easter dress to movies at the Paramount. And I hope I never leave the neighborhood or the parish. It's heaven on Earth."

In our office, all during the three-month so-called training program, Barbara gave me thumbnail snapshots of everyone in every department where I was supposed to learn the ropes.

"I'm terrified," I told her, "that I'll flunk the exam to get registered as a broker. (Today the basic test is called the Series 7.) I never even took second year algebra in high school. I was allowed to waive it and take art. My math skills are pitiful."

"You know what a schmuck is?" Barbara asked me.

"Of course," I said. "You don't have to be from New York to know what a schmuck is."

"Well," she said, "pay attention. You take the exam in the office. You got a problem, the brokers around you give you the answer. Nobody flunks. The firm doesn't hire you and have you flunk. *Capiche?*"

This was a surprise to me.

Barbara smiled. "We'll send you back to Boston with an education."

After our tour we went back to Manhattan and ate at a small gin mill near the New York Stock Exchange. It was a place the "runners" went after work, the messengers who ferried stock certificates all over the district, picking up and dropping off.

"I love today," I told her.

"It's an education on the streets," she said. "You grow up here, big families, everyone workin' hard, all kinds of people. But we pull it together. You can learn the business. You can learn to like Manhattan clam chowder better than New England. But learn to get real as you work down here, lunch with the big guys, fine. But drink and play with my friends who keep the engines going. Sharpen those elbows. Stick up for yourself. Learn to be a little more Brooklyn. Ruffle up the smooth stuff. You'll have a helluva career."

I've learned more about life from the traders and runners and the Damon Runyon characters than I *ever* learned from investment bankers and the boys in the "C Suites."

LEARN TO BE A LITTLE MORE BROOKLYN.
YOU'LL HAVE A HELL OF A CAREER.

21 | MOTHER

It would be difficult, I think, for a man to write a book about women, without talking about his mother and the lessons she taught. My mother needed a social life, to be around people, and, eventually, the type of mom who all my friends, and my little sister's friends wanted to be around, shooting the breeze in her kitchen. She was a child of the 1920s, the quintessential flapper. What's a flapper? The Oxford dictionary says, "From the 1920s ... a young, unconventional, or lively woman."

My mother may have been the first Jewish American Princess of the Boston suburbs. There were very few Jews at all in the Boston suburbs right after World War I when my grandfather built his brick house right in the middle of the Brahmin gentry. My grand-mother, Rebecca, who spoke with the accent of her original Polish village, was determined, as many immigrants of her generation were, that her children would be Americanized as swiftly as possible. My mother took ballet lessons, piano lessons, singing lessons. She took elocution lessons also, which included practicing different dialects, as if she would be telling jokes in an Italian accent, English accent, Italian and French. Here are a few pages from her high school diaries, which my own daughter inherited and cherishes:

February, 1924

> More snow than you can possibly believe; drifts up to my chest. The boys and Pa put the chains on the Oldsmobile and off we went to school. We stopped many times to pick up kids walking and we ended up with twelve in the car, everyone jammed up to the roof, and all of us eventually singing songs like "Tea for Two" and "It Had to Be You," at the top of our lungs with Pa singing louder than anyone. In algebra class, I told Miss Perkins that I'd much rather be singing with two people on my lap than doing algebra that I'd never use. After class I had to wash the blackboards and Miss Perkins told me I was "bad for morale." Algebra basically stinks …

Our daughter was 17 when my mother died, peacefully in her sleep at age 79. She had called me that afternoon, a Sunday, to complain about the New England Patriots game on television. "The other team can't tackle around the neck, can they? Isn't there a penalty for tackling around the neck?" Then she launched into, "Speaking of the neck," she added, "I met a woman at painting class who told me that if you try to stretch your tongue to reach the tip of your nose, and do it 50 times a day, you can lose your double chin."

"God, Mother," I said.

Years before, in high school, a friend said to me, "You know, I always thought your mother's name was 'God, Mother,' because that's what you said whenever she zinged you." And she went down zinging, which is what I hope for myself, particularly at the end, something like what Oscar Wilde supposedly said while dying in a seedy Paris hotel room. Staring at the impossible wallpaper, he gasped, "One of us has *got* to go."

My friends also said that mother was a "hot ticket," a big compliment at the time, since many of my friends' mothers were first generation Americans and decidedly strict in their mothering. She would take me shopping for clothes when it was time for back to school. Never to a traditional store. Always to a variety of small factories in Boston, pants makers, sports jackets, underwear, socks, shoes. It would take hours. Not just choosing the merchandise. That was fairly easy. As long as Mother made all the final choices. What took so much time, aside from traipsing to the various manufacturers (who only sold to retail customers if they were "connected"), was schmoozing with the owners, playing what my family always called "Jewish geography." This involved discussing parents, children, who got married, who died, and who lived next to whom in the tripledecker two houses ago, years ago, before they really made it in life and moved to a single-family house. As I grew older I dared to tell my mother how I hated almost all the clothes she bought for me. I remember one particular black and white, small-checked sports jacket she bought me when I was in high school and going to Sweet 16 parties.

"This looks like something out of *Abbott and Costello*," I said to her.

"Don't be afraid to be ahead of your time," she told me. "In a while everyone will be wearing these." But if I came home and described something I really wanted, a blue denim zippered jacket that all the guys were wearing and said, "Everyone is wearing this jacket," Mother would invariably say after a slight hesitation ... "All those people are jerks. What do *they* know?"

"I'll look like an idiot," I said.

Mother dismissed this, waving her hands at it. "Don't go where the crowds go."

My very first car, the Volkswagen Bug, had no heat and an accelerator pedal that was shaped like a round, large ball bearing.

Mother had found out about the car's arrival in advance. She called the dealership and ordered a small red pinstripe to be painted across the doors. "The right touch," she said to me when I first glimpsed the Bug. It's a legacy I preserve to this day as every car I've had since then I've had a thin colored stripe painted on the sides.

When mother was in her late seventies, she visited my uncle, her brother, at his beach house. She hated to have any pictures taken of her in a bathing suit. But my uncle Howard was a prankster. He shot several pictures of her in his backyard, sunning herself on a chaise. I have one of those snaps pinned to a bulletin board in my office. It's there to remind me of many things. My mom is grinning, her middle finger on her right hand pointed straight up in the air, giving the bird to her brother.

DON'T GO WHERE THE CROWDS GO.

22 | A BILLIONAIRE'S STREET SMARTS

I know one of the richest women in the world. Quite often, we pass each other on the sidewalks of our city. We stop and exchange greetings. She never takes herself seriously. But she takes the important things in life extremely seriously. Like family, and philanthropy, and new ideas. Common sense as well.

I've tried, in this book, to absorb wisdom about many subjects and professions from women of all ages and occupations. I've felt also, that the life lessons from these women could only be learned from them, that their take on the world is unique to them, presented to me over many years. It's advice that I've only heard from women. Because men seldom, in my experience, delve into the personal side of people and their problems.

Upon meeting this woman, you would never guess that she was anything but a woman of modest means. She dresses to feel comfy, not to impress anyone. If she wears jewelry, it is simple. She's kind and generous of spirit and greets newcomers always with a smile, almost as if she were a social worker.

But there's a steely side to her too, a decisive person who never hesitates to take control of a situation. She serves on many boards, and a friend of mine who is on one of those boards told me the story.

"Four of us," he said, "including the woman you admire who was our leader, were on a search committee to find someone to run our library, a private library which really is also a museum. It's also one of the most beautiful buildings in America, with roots that go back over 100 years, a major institution that we wanted to bring into the 21st century. One of the finalists ran a library at a fine small college in the western part of the state, and had a great reputation there, according to her résumé. One day, as the committee was drilling down on the candidates, our leader said, 'I've hired a van for tomorrow morning. We're traveling to the college tomorrow. We're going to poke around as if we were tourists, see what we can find out behind the curtain of management and résumés.'

"At the college," my friend told me, "we came on the spur of the moment, but the candidate wasn't there. 'This was on purpose,' our leader said. 'We're going in as if we're spies.' We talked to professors and department heads and janitors and security guards and receptionists. We told the people at the library front desk that it was on our 'bucket list.' The folks at the library were thrilled to get such eager visitors." He went on, "We got the grand tour from several librarians. We talked with security people, a docent who went on about the art collections. We were even invited to lunch. But we refused ... 'that would be a bit much,' our leader said."

All in all, they met and chatted with ten or more people, including students who were studying in the library. They checked the morale and enthusiasm of the employees. They specifically asked almost everyone about the current head librarian, one of them even asking someone, "Do you think she reads a lot, herself?"

"Oh, my yes," was the answer.

They spent about two hours at the library then got in the van and drove the four hours back home. "We felt like MI5 spies," my friend said.

I loved this story, almost as if the committee were, "search commandos." They explored the candidate in such an original way that I believe it never could have occurred to a man, it's just too unconventional. Contrast this with another friend of mine, high up in the "headhunter's world," searching for CEOs in the investment business. He told me, "a busy person reading a resumé for a hire at almost any company, will spend *16 seconds* looking at your credentials." The billionaire's search is much more detailed. But the *whole* person is almost, in my mind, never discovered with standard hiring methods.

I would hire the woman who is one of the richest in America in a heartbeat. She can teach everyone a few tricks.

The head college librarian got the new job, never knowing about the "road trip" by the spies.

TAKE THE TIME TO THINK IN UNCONVENTIONAL WAYS.

23 | DON'T BRING WINE

Of course, we understand from the earliest memories of life, how nurturing women are when we are nursed at our mother's breast. But what lessons can men learn from this and that special love that only grandmothers seem to offer to their grandchildren, love untainted by the many issues parents bring to the table.

When my wife Susan died, I was warned by many friends about the "casserole ladies," women, especially widows, who would deliver food to the grieving husband, some of them eager for companionship themselves, perhaps with ulterior motives.

That was the myth.

In my experience, in every case, the food delivered, including casseroles, were made or bought, and presented completely with caring and generosity of spirit. No guy ever delivered a bottle of Scotch, which to me, would've been a lot better than the clichés about

101

"better places," which many men offered to me as solace.

I counsel a lot of young people, the millennials, about branding themselves, how to separate themselves from this crowd of 330 million Americans. How to present yourself as a little different from others, not in peculiar ways, but in more original and caring fashions. Most of these lessons I've learned from women in my life, lessons that give us pause, or make us smile.

I rented a house recently for a two-week vacation, a place in California I've been visiting for years. My landlord is a bachelor, an organized man who pays attention to details and always leaves me a "cheat sheet" listing when cleaners are due, how to use the TVs, the tricks of the house on one sheet of paper.

This year he's been ill and could not help easing me into the rental's quirks. But there was his girlfriend, tending to him as a patient and making sure I remembered how everything worked in his house. When I carried my suitcase in, there were two big bouquets of fresh flowers in vases, on tables in the living room. *Home* is what they said to me. Very, very few men would have thought of something that welcoming. *Would he push the heat too high?* is what the guy might think.

If you're a man alone, a widower, a bachelor, in between relationships, the fresh flowers story makes me realize that, more and more, we men have to start thinking more like women if we're going to survive the new era I see all around us. What women do naturally, we have to learn and adapt and realize, like the old hit song from the 1950s, "Little Things Mean a Lot."

My friend Cinda refers to herself as a "California kid." Her family originally moved there from St. Louis after the Gold Rush days. She loves the little touches that can make one's approach to life a work of art. "For hostess gifts, I open up my bag of tricks," she says. "I give Meyer lemon hand cream. I even bring bags of small perfect Meyer lemons themselves. Or some lavender, or spices, things they can use up."

"I hate bringing wine," I told her. "So many people I know either really know wine, or pretend they do. I have no palate. No nose for it. Friends will disdain what I bring or re-gift it."

"Well," Cinda says, "if you want to wow the hostess, bring an over-the-top dishtowel, something outrageous printed on it, or violently colorful, or from some exotic place. For some reason, hostesses love to get dishtowels. Some call them tea towels. And if a man brings one, they'll never forget it. They'll tell their friends what an unusual man you are. It can lead to more invitations." I can tell you the dish towel idea really works.

"How the hell did you think of this?" friends say. "Well, I tell them, I have a lot of woman in me."

LITTLE THINGS DO MEAN A LOT.

24 | THE DENTIST

Millie is a dentist, a periodontist. Her real first name is Milagros. It means "miracles" in Spanish. "It's a miracle that I'm a periodontist in Boston with three children," she told me, "a little kid from Moca in Puerto Rico, about 80 miles from San Juan."

She is *my* periodontist. Once you have a perio person in your life, there's no such thing as one visit that takes care of you forever. No. Once you've entered that special world you're there for life, an annuity.

My periodontist for 25 years was a man I met on the squash courts. He eventually had my mother and sister as patients as well, all of us afflicted with gum disease. The old joke, "Your teeth are fine. But your gums have to come out," applied in our family. My sister railed against the gene pool. Mom and I accepted our fate quietly.

After many years on his feet, caring for his large and loyal patient list, our dentist retired and sold his practice to Millie. It turned out to be a fractious process, with Millie fighting to retain the patient list, proving to each new relationship that she was worthy of their trust, with no help from the former owner who, like many men facing retirement, deciding that he couldn't really face it, and hated the idea of losing his center. He's not alone in this.

My mother taught me to never make snap judgments, to always give the new teacher or new boss, or new doctor, a chance to prove themselves. "New relationships take time to develop. Maybe the only time snap judgments may work is in battle."

After I was Millie's patient for about a year, she told me about her early life. "A simple village, a simple time," she said. "Family and work, and a bit of church, when the girls were dressed as nuns and the boys as little choirboys. We all carried tiny wooden crosses." She still speaks with the flavor of her homeland in her accent. "I don't really speak English," she says, "today I speak dentistry." I asked her, "Where did the idea of dentistry ever pop up?"

"Well," she said, "my father drove a cab. My mother worked in a factory, sewing women's pajamas. She made all of our clothes. My dad drove a cab, up at 5 a.m., home about 4 o'clock in the after-noon. He'd put four people in the back of the cab, three in front, charge them 35¢, 40¢, go all day, maybe make $20 ... but that was good at the time.

"What was not so good was that my dad was a tough father. I had two sisters, three of us. But Dad thought he had three boys; he used to punch us if we misbehaved. That was the way. I love him."

Millie told me, "We learned a little English in school. But spoke nothing but Spanish at home. Today kids are on the Internet and they can't speak Spanish. Many jokes in life, all on us."

I asked about early education in Puerto Rico.

"I felt uncomfortable in school," Millie said. "Always feeling I was in the wrong place. Breakfast was a little piece of bread from a store my uncle owned, bread and a glass of Tang, four cents for breakfast. Lunch usually white rice and beans, Spam ... or corned beef out of a can, with a powdered milk called Klim. I began high school in our town. Every day I had to walk under a bridge on the way and older kids would spit down on us from above, and make fun of this skinny girl ... me. But I felt, all of this time, that there was something different out there for me. We had an uncle in Texas, with eight kids. My folks arranged for me to live with them in Austin, after I nagged them for months, wanting to get to the US and away from our small town. In Austin, I went to Sam Houston High School. The English language came slowly, we actually spoke Spanish in school. That's it. But I ran track, the 100-yard hurdles, now I think, typical, I pick the tough choice, run and jump, and you get a double whack if you bang into the hurdle and fall on the track."

Millie is always serious when she tells her stories, furrowing her brow.

"Another hurdle," she said, "a family member tried to assault me ... and kept trying and I'd fight him off. My uncle was hard on me too. He'd never let me date. The family would go out to parties. They'd leave me home with chores, like Cinderella. I'd listen to music and dream my dreams."

Millie went to college in Puerto Rico, with no idea what career path to choose. "All I knew was that I was great in biology and other sciences. But a friend dragged me to a 'job day,' at school where a dentist spoke about his practice. He said it was an eight-to-four job. Once you got your license, people would line up around the block to see you. I was so naïve and had seen my parents work so hard. 'That's for me,' I thought. 'I'll be a dentist. The easy life.' Not so easy, as I found out. In Puerto Rico, dental appointments were a pretty loosey-goosey enterprise. People would line up to see a dentist at 6 a.m. to get out a piece of paper that says in effect, 'show up at 8 a.m. to see the dentist.' Then they'd show up at 11 a.m. We don't believe in appointments. Dentists didn't believe they'd show up in time, either. They'd arrive for a 10 o'clock appointment at noon. Then it became 'first come, first-served.' You had a number, like in a delicatessen. Your number is called, and you come in. But it didn't mean much.

"I've told you I was so naïve. I now realize that you never know until you're in something. No one can tell you about marriage or raising children until you're in it. Books about the subjects don't mean a thing. On-the-job is the only way to learn."

She started dental school in Puerto Rico, in San Juan, and had a professor who flunked her in physics. "I learned early in Texas about young women out in the world and who preys on them. This professor of physics flunked me on tests and he'd give me private tutoring. I said I was naïve. I thought teachers and priests were people to admire. In his classroom he tried to attack me. I'll never forget him saying, 'I may be old, but I have feelings. I love you.'

"I went to the dean. 'No trouble,' said the dean, and I ended up with an A in physics. Deserved, by the way. When I graduated, the dean said, 'I'm so happy you're leaving. The hombres don't like the boats rocking.'

"In those days," Millie said, "you didn't rock the boat. You're a woman. You're a second class citizen."

She applied to dental school in the States, to NYU and flew there for an interview. "I had to borrow clothes for this from a cousin in New York. I was accepted. But then came the borrowing. Sallie Mae, the government. I needed $30,000 for classes and equipment. I knew I'd be a slave for years, paying it back. We also had to buy teeth to work on ... $3.99 per tooth. We had 13 Puerto Ricans in my class. We fed each other beans and rice for four years, and my dad sent me $100 a month." She went to work, after daily classes, on the 69th floor of the Chrysler Building, working on poor patients who came in from ten at night till eight in the morning to stay in school and support herself. All night ... and more classes and study during the days. She still didn't speak much English.

"I was in the middle of surgery at some point and the NYU book-keeper called me, saying 'You can't graduate, you owe us $12,000. Pick up your stuff. You have to leave.' The patient in my chair who

I was kind to, said, 'I'll pay your bills. Keep going on my gums.' I did, and *he* did. Again, a miracle."

I stayed with Millie as a dentist and she became a teacher about the way to run a personal business in the digital age.

She treats the whole person in her patients. She asks about your family and your past, and the pressures of *your* profession on *you*. She explains that oral hygiene can also be associated with chronic diseases like heart disease and diabetes, and for men, periodontal disease can also affect the prostate.

This gingivitis, inflammation leading to all kinds of maladies is much more prevalent in men. This is partly because more men than women ignore signs of plaque or bleeding gums, and as one male patient told Millie, "We just suck it up."

She gives her patients her cell phone number, wanting to know when they feel in distress. "I have three children," she tells me, "I know about what worries families, and what can lessen their anxieties. I feel I have to pay attention to what they fear, and help them over the bumps of being scared of dentists. Often what they are bottling up is fear of so many other things in their lives, aside from their mouths."

I've been Millie's patient now for about ten years. She has taught me and reinforced her emphasis of treating the whole patient, in my profession, the "whole client." She's more than a dentist, She's a social worker and a therapist.

Last year I had the biggest business year in my life. A great part of the reason for this is trying to bring the compassion of a woman like Millie to my own interaction with my clients and friends. If I still have success after 60 years of advising people about their money, it's because of women's advice to me over a lifetime about dealing with everything in people's lives. Not just about their financial well-being.

But Millie also says, "If your profession or job is tough, you need something outside of family and work. Something that takes you out of your self."

In two months recently she ran in four marathons: Chicago, the

Marine Corps in Washington, DC, Berlin and Athens. She has also run New York and the mother of them all, Boston.

DEAL WITH THE WHOLE PERSON, NOT JUST THE MEDICAL OR DENTAL ASPECT OF THEIR LIVES.

25 | THE EX-PATRIOT

Joan is an ex-pat who has lived in Rome for years. She paid a recent visit to me, coming to my office like a small whirlwind, full of energy and smiles. Joan is a client who was referred to me by another woman who spends at least five months in Italy every year. During Joan's time with me, I asked her about her life and how she faced the crossroads of divorce and living alone away from America. Her response underscored for me the bedrock that women represent and how much men could benefit by her creative approaches to her own life.

I'm sharing it with you, her words:

"The basics begin with family since that force continuously supported all my interests. In the horizon of the family my polar star was my noble maternal grandmother.

"Anna Mott Chuckrow arrived in New York City from Russia

in the 1860s; her harsh patriarchal father, one of the first rabbis in NYC, arranged a marriage she did not want (she loved someone else), sent her upstate to Troy, New York, where she, with her father's student, bore 11 children. Her husband died young leaving her with a large family. But this resourceful and much loved (by everyone!) lady created out of her home, a thriving chicken and egg business. She was noted for her positive wise wisdom and charity for the local poor. That business became the foundation for my uncles to create an empire, supplying much of the eastern seaboard and the US military with eggs during World War II.

"Her spinster daughters became successful businesswomen and my mother pursued education. She was in the first graduating class of SUNY, in Albany in the 1920s and as a graduation present the family gifted this shy, single girl with a ticket on the Queen Mary to travel around Europe. No one in my family felt marriage was a premium for a woman. When I finished college as an art history major, I married (someone I loved), had my own children and pursued my artistic interests by designing and making jewelry. We moved to Italy in the early '70s where my *then* successful screenwriter husband, my daughters and I had a rich life in this exquisitely historical city.

"Then came the darkness in the mid-'80s. I was confronted by a series of challenges: my husband decided to leave our family (with no money left in the bank for anyone), my daughters went to college (Dartmouth) in America, most of my jewelry was stolen in a bank heist (400 pieces), both my parents died and I needed to move from my apartment in Rome's historic center. For two years I lived in this dark time, confused and stunned. With my background I never went into bitterness or the 'poor me' syndromes. I was trying to figure out what I wanted, where I wanted to live and how to find my authentic me. Facing enormous issues in life, tips or formulas might pale. Often I think events that cancel what you assumed was your perfect life, force you to find the new reality.

"I started doing yoga exercises in the '60s when the first Indian gurus passed through the Yale campus (we lived there five years).

In those days America was changing with SDS (Students for a Democratic Society), students following Dr. King, the emergence of exposure to India (Krishnamurti: *Truth is a Pathless Land*) and general breaking of the American class structure.

"Growing up in freezing New York state, I pursued figure skating seriously, skiing recreationally, and modern dance artistically. Regular exercise was part of life for its pleasure and without realizing it then, the discipline that polishes knowing. My early exposure to yoga certainly was superficial but the seed was planted. Years later, in Rome, I met B.K.S. Iyengar, the famous 20th-century teacher, who directed me to deepen my abilities with his first teachers in London in the '70s. From then I taught as a hobby along with making jewelry. Later I studied with most of the great teachers in India and Europe.

"When my world demolished into a black pit (cannot find a better description), regular yoga practice given by these excellent teachers kept me mentally and physically strong. Yoga, practiced over 50 years, has taught me to be brave with life. It became a flashlight to move out of doubt, not for self improvement or stability, but as a way of life: Do. Be the best of your abilities, interests, be selective with your time and friends. I firmly believe in the kind of yoga that helps authentic growth with a gradual personal practice tailored to each individual. Over the years my interest has become specialized toward complimentary work with doctors for Parkinson's, sterility, cancer.

"So here is what I propose to you dear life helper, John. Women are more resourceful 'because they have had to be', as Simone de Beauvoir aptly stated in *The Second Sex*. I have taken lots of your time to give you highlights of my life but everyone has illnesses, losses, hardships on their own. No system, no advice no predictions can be valid unless each one deals with their own life in their own way. The process of living fearlessly, positively, tenderly and fully is part of the world and sharing all we learned about it! Men, if they are sensitive, can do the same as women.

"PS: Whoops I forgot … You asked about children. Family and children live their own lives. I sincerely hope I do not live my life through them. My attitude is 'I'm here for you when you need me.' I keep contact weekly (phone, emails) and avoid anything that would create a barrier for them and me."

———

Women put *feelings* into their lessons. They teach me compassion on my choices with people, and men have to learn to develop this skill. I *know* it makes me more successful in business.

What a gift to me from Joan. How she meets each day; her honest self knowledge, her humanity. I had never heard the Beauvoir quote before Joan mentioned it.

But last year I was talking to Diana who has helped us with house cleaning for 20 years and has had to deal with tough stuff in her life that I hope none of you ever have to endure.

When I spoke to her one day about my sense that this is "women's time," and about the real strength I see from my women friends in every arena, she just nodded her head and I left for work.

When I came home from work that day, I found a yellow sticky note on the wall above my sink. It said, *"We're strong because we have to be."*

YOGA BECAME MY FLASHLIGHT AS A WAY OF LIFE.

26 | A GRANDMOTHER'S FABLE

This spring, on the cusp of summer, I was taking a walk along a boardwalk in an old New England community near New Bedford. Spring had never really appeared this year, but that day the sun was out, and the residents, starved for melatonin were out in force, stopping on the walks every once in a while to hold their faces up to the sun.

Two women walked toward me, one older, in a one-piece bathing suit. She was covered in a large beach towel which had "Campobello" printed on one side in red. Her companion looked to be in her mid-twenties, in a blue bikini, a towel wrapped around her waist.

As they got closer, I knew them, a grandmother and a granddaughter, swapping family stories and secrets. "Happy spring," said the grandmother. She introduced me to her granddaughter, who smiled and held out her hand.

"Four months of winter, this year," I said waving at the sunshine. "About time." I looked at their towels, wet around the edges. "Don't tell me you went in the water."

"Of course we went in the water," the grandmother said.

"Yeah, she's amazing," said her granddaughter.

"This early in the year," I said. "I stick my toes in the water; it's freezing. I'll keep going, inch by inch, it's freezing. I always think I'm going to have a heart attack. It must take me ten minutes. A lot of times, I just turn around and take a walk."

"Well," Grandma said, "I just jump right in. All my life, whatever it is, I jump right in. Never had a heart attack." She paused. "What do you do for a living?"

"I manage people's money," I said.

"Boy, you must be very conservative. Sometimes in life, a cold shock, jumping in or jumping off, can be just the right thing."

The grandmother was right. There were a lot of times in my life where I should have "jumped right in." Men who stick their toes in gently, should pay attention.

JUMP RIGHT IN.

27 | THE UNSPEAKABLE

I have dear friends in deep mourning. Something unspeakable happened to one of their children and they had to receive counsel from a chaplain at one of Boston's largest hospitals. The chaplain was a Latina woman. They told her, "We're not going to get any comfort from religious messages." Not gracelessly, just that they didn't follow any organized, traditional faith.

"Oh, that's fine with me," the chaplain said. "I'm just a radical Argentinian Catholic."

That made them smile and they relaxed a bit with her, sensing someone who understood the human condition, including grief. She said to them, "Keep it *small*. Every day, a smile, a belly laugh at something, a drink with a neighbor, a dinner with old friends. Keep it *small*." My friends were able to take their nightmare down from cosmic, to a part of their daily activities and to look forward to little joyous bits and pieces that took them away from the ache in their hearts. "It was the best, smart advice we have ever gotten from anyone, delivered with such grace and understanding. She was an incredible gift to us. The idea of the bits and pieces of things that connect us to others keep us going."

KEEP IT SMALL.

28 | THE RABBI'S WIDOW: PLAYING IN THE MUD

I believe in the accidental nature of life: who walks into the room at the right time or the wrong time and changes certain things forever. If we are *out there* and open to new adventures, good accidents can and will happen.

At a wedding in Maine recently, I was seated next to a woman I had never met. I was told that her husband had died several months earlier, and that he had been the rabbi for one of the biggest congregations in the Midwest. She had been told that I had lost my wife as well. Betsy looked to me like a fortune teller, focused on our conversation, screening out the music and the merriment around us. We talked of grief and mourning. "I mourned *before* my husband died," she said. "He had Alzheimer's for over five years. You mourn every day if you're the caregiver." Betsy had answers and solutions, *not* questions. She had a creative approach to every problem we discussed. She has two daughters. We talked about our kids. "Our girls were very different," she told me. "One was a real student, great grades, great scores. Her sister was the adventurous one. She wanted to travel, to be out there, in real-life, not books. And parents, you know, want to be equal to all their kids. Tough to do sometimes."

The brainy sister went to Yale. The adventurous sister went to the University of Illinois. The difference in tuitions was about $25,000.

"With the $25,000, we paid for our youngest to travel the world," she said, "learned to be independent, to keep her eyes and ears open. Her travel was her graduate school. Today she works for McKinsey." Betsy creatively made it come out even.

I get up every day wanting to learn something new. Betsy's approach to her children was unconventional and smart. Street smarts, my favorite kind of wisdom.

We talked a lot about loss and mourning, even staying in our seats when all the guests were bouncing up and down to "Celebration," and "Old-Time Rock and Roll."

Betsy has been a landscape designer for many years. "My salvation after Phil died was going into my big backyard, bordered by woods … and playing in the mud. In the weeks after he died, and pondering the universe by myself, one day it was pouring down rain. I put on my slicker and my boots and went out to pick up branches torn off by the storm. The rain and wind kept slamming down and I had no idea how long I stayed outside. But when I came in I felt at peace. I was happy out in nature. Playing in the mud."

Several weeks later I contacted the mother of the bride at that wedding, asking for Betsy's email address and phone number. When she answered the phone I said, "If I want to learn something new every day, I think you can give me *months* of material."

She surprised me. "I've been thinking about you. I sensed that you were full of angst. I called a friend of mine, a psychologist who lives in an old Victorian house. She could help you a lot, I think."

I can't remember anyone in my life who has ever suggested that I seek counseling (even though I would never have written this book if I didn't need a lot of help ... with almost everything).

Betsy went on. "But the psychologist called me after our conversation and said, 'I Googled him and I guarantee he doesn't want to see me.'"

"Well," I said to Betsy, "don't judge a book by its cover. But I'm touched that you took the trouble to do such a thing."

"When my husband and I would meet someone we found interesting" she said, "we'd ask them to come to dinner. People love to be in each others' homes. In that setting, they're much more likely to open up about experiences and the things they've learned."

So I went for dinner, with a bottle of wine and an autographed book for her daughters. Betsy had already opened a bottle of her own wine. "I have cases and cases in the cellar," she told me. "Phil could never order anything in small amounts, wouldn't buy a bottle of something if he could buy a case. God knows, how many of those bottles have spoiled already."

"Speaking of God," I said, "you seem more like a wife of a pioneer in a wagon going through hostile country, heading west, doing everything. Not the wife of a clergyman."

She laughed a little. "My father disinherited me when I married Phil. He didn't want me marrying a rabbi. After we were married, we moved to Jerusalem and I studied Hebrew," she told me. "I think we were on the cusp then of what was expected of rabbi's wives. Forever, we were supposed to be the 'little woman' respectfully in back of our husbands, cooking, mothering, playing second fiddle at best to all the congregants, particularly their wives. Well, I was a Cleveland girl, and determined to be myself, not what someone thinks I should be; a secondhand citizen, wringing my hands. Nope."

Betsy loves stories, as we all do. "I was a pretty good golfer as a girl, but I hadn't played in years. One time, Phil's temple in the suburbs organized an outing, with golf, for the biggest givers to the temple. I played with three wives, determined that I would not play 'client golf' and defer to them. I'd play my own game, let the chips fall where they may. Nine holes, I was *one* over par. The three wives never spoke to me again. By the way, this attitude also extended to our children. Your kids shouldn't outdo the kids of the congregation. Local papers report triumphs of kids in the town: honor rolls, prizes, sports champs. One of our daughters coxed the US Women's National crew. I couldn't put it in the paper. Your kids shouldn't beat the congregation kids. Unwritten rules."

"How did you handle going outside the norms of your husband's profession?"

"We were both generals," Betsy said. "But we really reflected the separation of church and state. Remember, I'm a Cleveland girl. We were raised to be tough intellectually, and that meant independence of thought. I went to Purdue for college, 15 Jewish students out of every 15,000. That helped toughen me up.

"You learn the many lessons of human nature from being married to a rabbi," Betsy says. "Phil took big chances with his sermons. He made people think. But, you have a congregation, you have to give people something to talk about, you know what I mean? People gossip about the clergy.

"Phil and I went to Jerusalem the night of our wedding. I did marry into tradition. But I wasn't traditional. For instance, at Christmas in Jerusalem, I dragged Phil out to sing carols. He knew what he was getting into. Forever, rabbis' wives had a role, second-class citizens. Until women became better educated. When we moved back to America, women weren't really in the workforce; they were still taking care of the house and the children. But from about 1965 on, things began to change. You'd think Phil would've dumped me. But we were open and honest with each other. 'Betsy was the best investment I ever made,' he would say. I could fix anything. I came from a long line of civil engineers. I built a car engine out of a model kit. I plastered the walls in our house; I could fix the sink and toilets. I didn't believe in paying for anything I could do myself. Phil would just say, 'Wake me when it's over.'

"I said that Phil would challenge the congregation. He was an intellectual and did not believe that everything Israel did was always right. Modern congregations don't want controversy. They wanted a dog and pony show."

"How did you become involved in landscaping?" I asked her that afternoon when the sun was beginning to fade.

"Well, the good life involves throwing yourself, I believe, into acts of goodness and this includes into areas that are not sedentary. I rode a bike in challenge race, after my daughter was diagnosed with breast cancer. The race raises money for research. I raised $25,000 and rode 100 miles even though I had never really attempted anything like this. It was hard, like real life is hard. When I first rode, I was 64 years old. But with my daughter's challenge, I needed one as well.

"Landscaping came from curiosity, signing up for a college seminar on the subject, and got a certificate which allowed me to start a business. In the class, I studied the history of Italian gardens and also the history of Chinese gardens, particularly in their mountains. The course opened my eyes to the differences in societies. In the mountains of China, the stories were of dragons protecting the people. In Europe, the dragons *ate* you.

"We had a huge back yard with a forest bordering it. A shady environment. It's more interesting to me," Betsy said. "The shady side of life. You can learn to accentuate what's already growing there and not bring in new plantings. I was 53 when I started the business, and only took referrals from others, no marketing except word-of-mouth. I would never take anyone from our congregation—conflict of interest. I already had too many targets on my back. One of them in the congregation said to me once, 'Where you live. How come you chose there? It's pretty fancy; investment bankers, hedge funds.'"

Betsy gave a little laugh. "Everyone kept telling me 'this isn't traditional; that isn't traditional.' I believed in starting my own traditions.

"My landscaping has saved me in many situations. One of my best friends died in North Carolina. When I got the news, I went out into the woods in back of my house and pruned several trees. In grieving, I was making something better. Interesting that at my Radcliffe courses many of the women in my classes worked in healthcare; nurses and physical therapists. They dealt with so many traumatic things each day, they were drawn to making something beautiful."

I've learned many lessons from Betsy. Here are a few that seem universal to me, and that can give us all food for thought:

1. When someone is hurting, the best thing you can do to help is the bringing or the sending of food. It means the most to anyone in distress or grieving, because they almost never have the time to think about this most essential of needs.

2. Betsy told me, "I was on a plane once from Vienna to Boston and I sat next to an Afghan man, who was thrilled now to be living in America. He told me, 'we will be at war forever in Afghanistan,' he said. 'the tribes, the warlords, the petty power struggles will never be gone. They go back 1,000 years. And it's not just our country, it's everywhere. Why do you think people keep pouring into America? Even though it also has its tribes. But the Middle East? Hate is so much easier than love.'"

   Betsy adds, "I see this in my travels. Recently in Chile, I walked down one street with all kinds of private clubs on it. Israel, England, France. People want to be with *their* tribe. It's human nature to mistrust others."

3. If you're going to run a company, or a condo association, or a board of directors, or *especially* a congregation, you'd better learn how to play hardball.

4. "I find that the best way to lead an interesting life that can make a difference is to ... do *preposterous*."

And she has.

FIND YOUR OWN THERAPY—GO PLAY IN THE MUD.

29 | THE GIFT THAT KEEPS ON GIVING

It's tough to believe that one can get good advice from the same person, or tips on life separated by 65 years. Dates in high school in the mid-1950s were pretty innocent, even though always fueled by fantasy, if you were an adolescent boy. Because so few of my friends had a car, double dating seemed to be the norm for me and my friends. Those friends were called "car buddies."

My friend Bobby had a car, and a regular girlfriend. Everyone had a nickname in high school. Bobby's was "Freaky," partially because his hobby was riding horses, not playing sports with the rest of the guys; football in the fall, ice hockey played on ponds in the winter, baseball in the spring. Freaky rode horses in a distant town. Nobody we knew rode horses. It was also rumored that, at summer camp, he slept with his eyes open.

My date was a first date for me. Anne, a classmate, tall and out of my league. I didn't even have a league. "She only dates college guys," other friends told me. Kids we thought were rich had fathers who owned a business, usually shoe or textile factories, manufacturing when Massachusetts was a power in manufacturing. Their fathers drove Cadillacs, the most visible outward sign of wealth. Or they had finished basements in pine paneling, maybe with a pool or ping -pong table. I never got a look at Anne's father's car or her basement.

The four of us went to a movie, *The Man Who Knew Too Much*. Doris Day was the female lead, singing "Qué Será, Será," one of the biggest hit singles of the year. After dinner, Freaky said, "We're going to Storyville. Listen to some jazz." I had never been to Storyville, one of Boston's early jazz night spots, founded by George Wein, who invented the Newport Jazz Festival, and a legend in the music business. There was a two-dollar cover charge at Storyville. Per person. We stayed for about an hour, nursing ginger ales. Anne had a Shirley Temple. "Of course *you* got a cherry," I said to the table, figuring Anne would always get something no one else had.

I didn't have what everyone else had when the check came ... the money.

The movies cost a total of four dollars. I had six dollars in my pocket at the beginning of the night. I knew it would be a bit tight, but I figured that Storyville would be a couple of bucks and some change. We heard Don Shirley make magic on the piano and, in between sets, I struggled with finding witty things to say to the girl who only dated college guys. I sprinkled a lot of "qué será's" into my conversation, and then Freaky asked for the check. It totaled about $12. Freaky Bobby seemed to have unlimited funds, and he knew why I was kicking him under the table. "We split it," he said, "even though Anne had two Shirley Temples." I had never heard of a "cover charge." I had never been to a club of any kind in my life. I also wasn't too acquainted with the subject of tipping. The ladies went to the ladies room. Our waiter brought the owner over to our table.

"Never heard of the cover charge, is that right?" he said to me.

"No clue, sir," I said. "Well," George Wein, the jazz legend said, "it's a cheap lesson for you. What's the Boy Scout motto? *Be prepared*. You've got a pass tonight. Empty your pocket and give it all to your waiter. Now you'll know forever what a cover charge is."

I thanked him and answered, "Qué será, será."

The ride home was a bit chilly. We were dropping off Anne first. I broke the silence by saying things like, "Don Shirley makes me wish I had kept up my piano lessons." Freaky's girlfriend was snuggled up close to him in the front seat. It was the days when there was no separation between the seats. Just like one long couch.

At Anne's house I got out of the car to walk her to her door. Halfway up to her front steps she reached out and briefly held my hand. "It's okay to be innocent about things," Anne said. "And being a wise guy doesn't mean that you really are."

For years, every time I heard a Doris Day song, I thought about that night and her kindness to a kid who had a lot to learn.

———

Sixty-six years later, Anne called me and asked if she could come into my office for lunch. She had done business with me sometime earlier, had left at some point and we had contact only when her husband invited me once a year to speak to graduate business students where he taught at Brandeis University. When she called me, it was several weeks before I was scheduled to lecture to students again. "It's been on my mind for a long time," she said, "to let you know why I left you. It's bothered me for years."

She never did tell me, other than saying, "It was one of the biggest mistakes of my life."

I asked her about her husband's family, who lived in Minneapolis, about as far away from Boston as the Earth is from the Moon.

"They're bedrock," she said. "No affect. No other agenda. They invite you in with goodwill and assume that that's what you'll give back as well." I knew that Chuck, her husband, had been a star high school football player who was heavily recruited by colleges and ended up at Harvard, who at the time had been destroyed by Yale 53–6, and Harvard was determined to never let that happen again. Recruitment exploded.

"Anne," I said to her, "you and I grew up in an almost completely Jewish environment in our town. Were you a stranger in a strange land, marrying into a Midwestern churchgoing family?"

Anne paused a bit, then said, "If you're lucky in life, you get to meet a few really incredible people; Chuck's mother was one of those."

Once in a while, someone will describe a person dear to them and their whole body language seems to open up in their admiration, from smiles to animated hand gestures.

"My mother-in-law," Anne said, "was the youngest of 13 children. She grew up on a farm, in a household where the father did not believe in education for women."

I believe in the accidental nature of life, who walks in the door at a particular time, who you never knew, and changes your life in wonderful ways. An accident, for instance, is how most married people met their spouse.

Chuck Reed came into my life some years ago. He initiated the graduate business school at Brandeis University, a program for foreign students. Chuck was the first dean of the school. Because of books and articles of mine, he invited me to speak to the students on life and the investment business.

Chuck came from a small town in Minnesota, an all-star football in high school, he was recruited by Harvard. Chuck had been raised in evangelical Christian, hard-core Midwestern home.

After I had spoken at Brandeis, the three of us had dinner. "How the hell did you two find each other?" I asked, because they came from such completely different backgrounds. They had both been divorced and met, not through the Internet, which had not been invented yet, but at a "social for divorced singles."

"An accident," they both said at the same time.

After dinner I invited Anne to come to my office for lunch, to catch up on the years since we'd seen each other. But also to chat about stock markets, in which she had strong interest.

At lunch I asked her about the concept of "opposites attract."

"Well," she said, "as you know, I grew up in a completely Jewish environment. But, for a few years I did go to an all-girls' school that had a really small minority of Jewish girls. So I was somewhat prepared for being a minority. I was also a day student which limited friendships in certain ways. I fell in love with Chuck, so strong and competent and good to me.

"Going to Minnesota to meet his family was scary, full of anxiety for me. But *anticipation* is so often much worse than the reality. 'Where will we stay in the house?' I asked.

"'We stay together.' He had gotten a letter saying that *'no'* we would not be staying together, and I did feel a coldness when I first arrived, that had nothing to do with Minnesota in the winter. It was Christmas and there was a piano in the parlor. All Chuck's family were there munching snacks, having drinks. So I went over to the piano and began playing Christmas carols and the pop songs too, 'Rudolph,' and 'Silver Bells,' and 'White Christmas.' Everyone gathered around and sang. Afterwards, I got up from my seat and pointed to my head. 'See,' I said … 'No horns.'

"It all broke the ice and I was part of the family. We did stay in the same bedroom.

"Chuck's mother was an unusual woman. She grew up in a small town of a thousand people. Her sophomore year in high school she left home, moved to a city, and got jobs. Then she got a teacher's degree and taught in a one-room school."

Anne went on. "I was always sort of a laissez-faire person. You know, live and let live. I have three children. A lot of us tend to bite our tongues with family or in business situations. Chuck's mother told me, 'no one asks anything personal, it would be an invasion of privacy. By never really asking questions in a family, no one really helps people in trouble. Always err on the side of intrusion.'

"That line," Anne said, "has changed my life with my children and my friends in ways I can never really emphasize enough."

It's also given *me* the courage to explore my own children's lives in, I think, helpful ways. It's also give me a new dimension in probing the real needs of my clients, finding out the truths behind the headlines of their lives.

ALWAYS ERR ON THE SIDE OF INTRUSION.

30 | HEPBURN

You and I know that the one thing any woman must understand about men is that they are all little boys. Some more than others, of course, and some keep it hidden better than their buddies but it's lingering there like the pimple you know is going to be showing on your chin by tomorrow morning.

My wife Susan had a great talent in this regard to cut through the nonsense. Years ago, I showed her a picture in a magazine. "Look at this woman," I said, pointing to a model in an advertisement. "I'm sure she's in her fifties and she's got shoulder length hair. Look how great it looks." Susan had her hair cut short at the time.

She looked at the picture, then at me. "Grow up," she said, and walked away.

She got it, and, of course, this drove me nuts from time to time. But there was a moment in my life when it was OK for boys to be boys, even though they were dressed like girls. My senior year in college I was one of the female leads in the Hasty Pudding show, a musical spoof written, produced, and performed annually since 1868 by male students, until just several years ago.

Jack Lemmon had acted in the show. And Fred Gwynne of *The Munsters*. And Bill Weld, former Governor of Massachusetts. Alan J. Lerner wrote a show, as did Erich Segal of *Love Story* fame. Traditionally, men played all the female roles, and there was always a kickline number that was brought back for at least two, sometimes three encores.

For years there had been a tradition of choosing a "Woman of the Year" at the Pudding, usually a famous actress, to get publicity for the show and have an excuse for a party in the middle of the day. That year, the honoree was Katharine Hepburn, who accepted her award (a small cast-iron pudding pot), on stage surrounded by selected cast members, including me in costume as my character, the Duchess of Wopping, complete with glamorous tiara set on top of golden curls.

Katharine Hepburn viewed the proceedings with wry amusement, the only real woman there, and the only woman, fake *or* real, in pants. After the photographs, she watched us sing a few numbers, including my big hit song, done with my husband, the Duke of Wopping. It was the "Abdication Waltz" and when it was over the great Hepburn took me by the arm and said, "Young man I strongly suggest when you graduate that you go to law school," which in more recent times would be "Don't give up your day job."

I asked her, hoping for show business goodies that I could tuck away, if she had any suggestions for us playing female characters. "Of course," she answered. "Read the female roles in Shakespeare. Everything you want to know about character and the theater is in Shakespeare."

The party moved into the bar for cocktails and music provided by the three-piece band whose members also played for the show's performances. Hepburn was surrounded by people at the party, all looking, like me, to impress her. The room was dark and oak-paneled, filled with old leather sofas and chairs sitting on even older oriental rugs. A long, curved bar dominated one wall facing a large oak mantlepiece that topped a fireplace. All the walls were covered with framed show posters dating back to the late 1800s bearing names like *The Big Fizz*, *Love Rides the Rails*, and *Bombastes Furioso*. Many of us in the musical had visions of show business careers after college, thinking that life, like the Hasty Pudding Club, would be all fun and games.

After a few drinks, the band blaring out "The Lady is a Tramp" and other songs likely played at coming-out parties, I decided to climb on top of the small upright piano. This would really let Katharine Hepburn see me strut my stuff so she would want to be my friend forever. The band struck up the kickline number, and two chorus members joined me on top of the small upright. The room was cheering up until one of my high kicks collided with a hip check from the dancing neighbor and I was launched off the piano into the band—actually through the bass drum with my head.

As I came up for air, the drummer began beating me with the sticks, yelling, "My *best* drum, my *best* drum," until we were separated and held apart. After things settled down, Katherine Hepburn, ready to leave the event, came over to me and smiled the star's smile. "I said Shakespeare's *heroines*, she counseled, not Shakespeare's *fools* ... " She gently tapped me on the hand with her little prize pudding pot and was gone.

So what did these adventures teach me, before I went off into the real job world? Two lessons will benefit you in your long careers to come: One, be mindful of the absurdities in life and how often they will occur; two, never take yourself too seriously. Almost every time I think I'm really smart, I get my tail handed to me.

OFTEN, IF YOU PLAY THE FOOL, YOU'LL BE TAKEN FOR ONE.

31 | ANTHEMS

My friend Pam lives in a big city, far away from mine. She has a particular knack for making friends with smart people. She's smart herself, and listens as well as she talks. She gets therapy on a regular basis from these friends, none of whom are professional therapists.

"My best friends," Pam tells me, "don't really know each other. I'm the common denominator. When I'm indecisive about certain things, and at crossroads, I'll lay it out, with honesty, to these smart best friends. Whenever they all agree on how to solve a problem, and I talked to them separately, I'll follow their advice.

"Occasionally though," Pam went on, "I'll grab onto something one of my friends does to uplift her life. Recently, my friend Dolly (after Dolly Parton), told me something that I loved. She's a doctor, and works with homeless people, thousands of them are served by the facility where Dolly works. Every day is really tough, like you can't believe tough. I don't have a big enough heart to have it broken everyday. So on days I feel particularly blue, I drive into the city and play the song 'Titanium' by Sia at the loudest I can play it. 'Sticks and stones may break my bones,' she sings, 'far away, far away' she sings. And for a while, it takes *me* away. I suppose I need a beat master in my life. Maybe we all do."

There are so many bumps in life we all face. There are many mornings none of us feel like going to work, because of the scary aches in our bellies about what may be waiting for us. It does help to have an anthem playing in our ears to go into battle. The Beach Boys can do it for me in the morning commute. Or, "American Pie."

I think we all need an anthem.

FIND YOUR OWN ANTHEM—AND SING IT OUT LOUD.

32 | THE ARTIST

If you choose the creative life for yourself, it can be a lonely path. I have many clients who are writers. A few are immensely successful. Most are bumping along, book to book, putting it out there, happy when good reviews appear. But almost always not getting what they think they deserve. I know that it's the same with actors, and dancers, painters and musicians as well. What seems glamorous is mostly glamorous from the outside looking in.

I do have several artist clients as well: painters, for the most part, as well as friends who paint as talented amateurs.

Then, there is my friend, Katherine Houston. She fits the description of my favorite people. She is "bent," not afraid to be deliciously unconventional. Katherine is a real life decorative artist. She does it for a living. Her lessons to me on what immersion in a creative life means, allows me to understand a woman whose nightly dreams often include shapes and designs and colors. Every week she picks a project and sticks with it.

If we're lucky in life, we hear "the click." Katherine's click occurred at age forty-seven. She was married to a doctor, had four children, and was living in London for a year, while her husband was part of a grant program in urology.

She grew up in Columbus, Ohio, and went to college at Michigan, majoring in art history.

"I went to Michigan because it was so large, I knew I could lose myself there and focus on anything I wanted to do. I could be that loner in a large crowd, just the place for me." The loner aspect of creativity comes with the territory. Her senior year at Michigan she took an oil painting class. The last project was supposed to be an abstract, like Braque, or Picasso, or Dufy. She hated abstract painting. "So I put together a joke. A mishmash of weird creatures, a nightmare painting that Dali would have called a pitiful imitation of his style. I showed it to my professor, gave him a good look at it. Then I tossed it in his wastebasket and walked out."

A week later, a friend called Katherine and said, "Congratulations, it's amazing."

"What is?" she said.

"You won first prize, the gold medal."

"My professor plucked my painting from the trash and entered it. It was a joke to me. I couldn't stand the painting. I did it as a total lampoon. I never did another oil painting ever again in my life. Or anything that you could call abstract. That wasn't me."

For the next twenty-four years she only used watercolors, painting just to amuse herself. Then, in 1986, at 47 years old, she and her husband rented a small flat in London. One day, they walked by a shop in Knightsbridge, owned by a decorator. In the window were several porcelain pieces, delicate fruits and vegetables. Katherine thought they were surely Chinese exports or Meissen or Sevres, the finest examples of that craft.

"They're wonderful," she told the owner, "where did you ever find

WAKE UP

them?" She thought they had to be 18th-century gems.

"No," said the owner. "They're actually done by a lady in Pangbourne, about an hour away."

"Do you think she would ever take on a student? Like me?"

"Knowing this lady, I highly doubt it. But I can ask her."

The decorator called the next day and said, "Anne Gordon, the artist, would like to meet you. She and *her* husband want you and *your* husband to come out for lunch."

It turned out that Anne Gordon was a true "Lady," the Marchioness of Aberdeen. Her husband was in the House of Lords, a Marquis, known simply as "Aberdeen." British aristocracy. At the lunch she and her husband were served cocktails, more cocktails, followed by wine, and classic roast beef with Yorkshire pudding.

After lunch, Lady Gordon gave Katherine an hour's tutorial in her porcelain techniques and ended up telling her, "There's no mucking about. There's no convenient time ever, to go to work. Just *do it*."

Amazingly, Katherine Houston did. Just like the sky opened and her life changed forever. She concentrated on studying 18th-century paintings of fruits and vegetables, modeled on the Dutch painters Frans Snyders and Jan DeHeem. Also the wood carver Gringling Gibbons. From these paintings she began to create pieces in three dimensions, working with as many as 300 different colors. She uses twelve to fourteen applications of low fire overglaze, whereas commercial porcelains only use one or two. The results are richly colored works that look like Dutch Master still life paintings, only in 3D. The colors never fade. Her flowers and vegetables sit on mantles and serve as centerpieces. They can be found in private collections, museums like the Peabody Essex, and in stores as varied as Gumps, Bergdorf Goodman and Neiman Marcus. I commissioned her to do a centerpiece for my dining room table. Parrot tulips; a thing of wonder.

How many people do you know who have had the sky open up one day, and because of it, completely change the course of their lives? I've never met anyone so focused on creating beauty that almost every paragraph they say to themselves, ends in how the next piece of porcelain is made. Does it have enough leaves? Am I using too many or not enough colors? Does it have a few tiny raspberries sprinkled amongst the parrot tulips?

Go search the artists she has drawn from. Now imagine these images in 3D, on your mantlepiece, or a centerpiece on your dining room table, or a sideboard. She does so much research on colors. When she began her porcelain journey she went to visit companies that produced paint for automobiles. She got through to Corning Glass Works and went to see their facility in Corning, New York. Their head of design research went over their techniques with Katherine. "Everyone who is serious about their work, I find, will respond to someone who is equally serious about their work in the same field. And almost all people respond to creations of beauty."

Katherine just turned eighty. Her birthday party in mid-COVID-19, consisted of her, her husband Ted, and me.

"What did you do with your special day?" I asked her.

"I went to my studio and spent a few hours solving a big problem in one of my pieces. Then I came home and had the pleasure of sitting on my living room sofa and reading Graham Greene." Katherine keeps a journal, a very old-fashioned notebook, full of advice for her grandchildren, the "Rules of Behavior," basic etiquette, and so much more, about cooking, and art and life.

"Tuck in your tummy, shoulders back."

"Write a thank you note to a hostess within three days."

"You are what you read."

"Try to live your life as if you're majoring in the novel."

She does something that I don't see many modern mothers doing with their children or their grandchildren. She is not shy with her advice. She doesn't want the younger generation to be her buddies. She will be outspoken, sharp of tone, not enabling them, or caring if she is tough. I've met many of her grandchildren. Instead of thinking of her as "The Wicked Witch," they seek her counsel and love her very much. Because she levels with them. They come to trust her criticisms and advice. She never fakes it. She doesn't want to be their "bestie." She want to set an example.

Her creative time is solitary in her studio in the South End of Boston. Assistants who work for her are not allowed to talk while she's creating.

But out in the world her social life is enriched by dozens of women, old and new friends, from schools and travel, and from just plain curiosity about people she has just met. She served on a jury in the last year, a murder trial. One of her fellow jurors lived near Katherine's studio in a district of Boston that is as mixed as a salad full of colorful veggies. Hispanic, black, white, gay, straight. The juror was a younger woman and Katherine was determined that they become friends after the trial. "Wonderful things," Katherine tells me, "can come from curiosity. You never know where you'll find kindred spirits. I always learn something from these friendships. Not just gossip or current events but book suggestions, and movies, and tales of peoples' lives from many different places."

On a break, Katherine saw the young juror reading a book. "Amazing," Katie said to her, "that's one of my all-time favorites." What book? It was *Warlight* by Michael Ondaatje. "I can't believe how much this book meant to me. It's possible to learn from new people every day, if you're curious."

The young woman has a map of Boston, which has every neighborhood in detail. She is determined to walk every street in the city and check off each one in her diary. How can you not be fascinated by someone like that?

And they were off, one book recommendation leading to another, and an agreement that they would meet for lunch after the trial was over. Which they did.

More recently, she had a doctor's appointment and found common ground about aches and pains with her doctor's nurse. They've made a lunch date.

"Ask people you meet about themselves, with honest interest. It will pay dividends in your appreciation of the diversity of the world."

This shows me that you can be immersed in humanity and be a loner at the same time.

But because of Katherine, I *don't* walk by security guards in my building, or parking attendants in garages, or people delivering mail, as if they're invisible. I'll ask them how they are, how they got their jobs. If they're immigrants, I ask about their home countries.

Someone called me recently, out of the blue, a friend of a good friend of mine. He was looking for a phone number or an email address for this mutual friend who had been in a long-term care facility, suffering from dementia.

"I've lost track of Mike," the stranger said. "I know you've been close for years. Can you put me in contact?"

I could have just given him the info. But, with Katherine's stories in mind, I asked the caller about his life. We talked for over a half hour as he told me that his lifetime love of baseball led him to a career switch as an entrepreneur, to moving to Israel where he coached the Israeli national baseball team for years. He got the job with pure chutzpah, having only coached as a rank amateur, with a high school team in a Boston suburb.

The stories I get from strangers, with a bit of curiosity and empathy, can connect you with extraordinary people, who can enliven your life with tales outside of your comfort tribe. It's how you can learn about the world, paying you dividends you never dreamed of. Try it, even if you cannot create delicate flowers and vegetables out of paper-thin porcelain.

But, I think, the biggest lesson Katherine offers, by example and never preaching, is to be truly great at something; it has to be the most important thing in your life.

IT'S OKAY NOT TO BE BUDDIES WITH YOUR CHILDREN AND GRANDKIDS. EDUCATE THEM.

33 | WOMEN AND THE PANDEMIC

The guys who are not working watch big screens and small screens, sometimes all day. These men are the retired cadre. Unless they have strong hobbies, like putting little ships into bottles, or holding magnifying glasses up to tiny stamps for their collection, they seem bored, and as we all do at one time or another, ask ourselves, "What's it all about?" And "Who am I?"

Many men are walking dogs, face masks in place, poop baggies hanging out of coat pockets. The men who *are* working really seem to miss their offices, too much distracting them at home. These men are not at all comfortable in their new subnormal life.

I'm running my business on the screen, also watching CNBC to fill the daily holes for what I may be missing using my own instincts. I am also secretly wishing that, as I'm watching, a cure for the virus will magically appear. Men tend to daydream like that. Will I make the team? Does she love me? Will I hit the lottery? And all day I reach out to my clients, texting them, calling them.

Periodically, every firm I've worked for would hire McKinsey or other large consultants, pay them millions, to answer one question. "What do the clients really want?" After shelling out millions, the answer was *always* the same. "We want our advisors to stay in touch with us, particularly in tough times. We want to hear from them."

So my partners and I and our support staff spend our days reaching out to all of our clients, large and small. "All life is relationships," is my life mantra.

But the men I talk with do not reach out to their men buddies by phone about personal matters. They respond to each other about the endless YouTube dumb and smart animal tricks. Or the salacious postings about politicians and celebrities, or memories from highlights of the 1950s. But they don't talk to each other about solace or advice or comfort. Women communicate one-on-one, and in virtual groups. They go outside and walk together, particularly when the sun shines and they can take in the vitamin D. They give each other therapy: tips on food, and cosmetics, on books read, shows and movies watched, children and grandchildren, and health stories. They congregate virtually in every manner available, including those walks. They're playing virtual bridge, and sending chain letters, the kinds that say, "if you don't send this on, there may be bad luck in the future ..." One of my women friends told me, "You know, real friendships matter. It's like the 23rd Psalm. 'It restoreth my soul.' Our friends' networks restoreth our souls."

No man is going to say that to me. No male friend is calling me to offer therapy or to tell me what hand lotion protects my skin after endless washings. Although five men texted me separately telling me to watch the Michael Jordan documentary. Oops. That's not completely right. A friend from Denver, a retired orthopedic surgeon, who I almost never hear from, called me this week and said, "I miss you. We never get enough time together alone to chat. How're you doing?"

I thanked him and said, "This is so sweet of you. And unexpected. Even better."

He paused and said, "Well, truth be known, my wife urged me to call you."

His wife is a child psychiatrist.

MEN, FORCE YOURSELF TO ACTUALLY PHONE OR TEXT YOUR MALE FRIENDS.

34 | READING THE ROOM

Dr. Lydia Shrier is a behavioral pediatrician. Lydia loves both of her parents. It's rare that I hear this from clients or friends, particularly if they're honest about it. She's at Children's Hospital in Boston. I met her 15 years ago when she married a client of mine, also a pediatrician at the same hospital. Lydia met him there. He is an expert on the media's influence on children. Lydia focuses on this as well, plus deals with eating disorders and all other ailments and fears of the adolescent.

"It's probably not an accident that I became a pediatrician," she says. "My mom is a doctor, a psychiatrist. Dad is an engineer. He always had been a lab rat. He was an energy expert often testifying to Congress. For a time he was president of the Exxon Solar Division.

"I went to a Montessori preschool and came home one day and

told my mom, 'I want to be a nurse when I grow up.'

"'Lydia,' my mom said, 'I'm a doctor. That's probably what you want to be shooting for.'" Lydia went on, "I went to a big public high school in Montclair, New Jersey, 1,400 kids in my class. It was half black and half white.

"I guess I was with the nerdy kids, math and science geeks. But from the time I was little, music was my escape from studies. I started with the trumpet first, then switched to the French horn. But I couldn't master the off beat, so I switched again, this time to the trombone. I flunked that one too. I did love music but it was really driven by my talent for math that kept me at it. Then, by accident, I found the euphonium, and that little horn became my dream instrument. Band competition was big in New Jersey, and our high school marching band was one of the best in the state. Not many people can say that music and math got me through adolescence."

The euphonium is like a baby tuba. Lydia played it in the marching band and in a jazz band in school as well. She went to Yale for college. "I was just fine academically," she says, "and had no reason to make a choice like Yale, whose mascot was a bulldog. It was totally whimsical, but our high school mascot was also a bulldog. Not a great reason to make my choice of colleges. But a lot of things in life are accidental. Random. Life can make us do ridiculous things from time to time. And ... you never know. I chose a rarified field of concentration, applied math and biochemical engineering, trying to meld the professions of my parents.

"There were only nine students at Yale in that double major. In med school I entered pediatrics," Lydia told me. "Some things can be ridiculously simple-minded to other people. I entered pediatrics because I liked kids. It was that simple.

"In my fourth year I found myself thinking about what an incredible journey it was, shepherding adolescents. No wonder the upper class in British society shipped their kids off to boarding school. Why would they want to be bothered with the *sturm und drang* of those often horrible years? I took triple boards in med school, two years in adult psychiatry, two years in pediatrics and two years in child psychiatry. But I'm very much a pediatrician. I have a primal need to feel that stethoscope bouncing on my chest. I want so much to practice medicine as well as treating the hope and fears.

"In those two years with adult psychiatry, I had a particularly tough time with one suicidal woman who had been in a Nazi concentration camp in Poland. I did not have the courage to handle that horror. Treating adults was not for me. But I did think I could bring children to the light."

Here's a snapshot of the most memorable lessons Lydia taught me:

1. With patients: be clear, direct and maternalistic. But be authoritarian in your delivery. I was seeing a young woman recently who had a nervous stomach and other symptoms of constant anxiety. She and her mother were both big believers in homeopathic solutions. At our first meeting, gathering information, I did not tell them that what they were doing was basically a crock of poop. It wasn't working. By our next meeting, I said to them both, "Can I be really honest with you?"

    "Of course," the mother said.

    "I'll make it really simple. You need *meds*." There was no equivocation in my tone. Nothing fuzzy. They grabbed for that simple message as if grabbing a lifeline. A light bulb went off. I told them how much I thought the young woman would benefit from medication. It succeeded and they thought I was a miracle worker. What I really was, was decisive. Patients, I have found over the years, want a cure. They want their doctor to be *the* problem solver. To be direct.

To me, it's a lesson in leadership. It makes me think about medicine and money management as well. Lydia's patients want solutions, not "let's try this and see if it sticks." They want a game plan for their problems, and someone who delivers it who is comfy in their own skin when it comes to the medical or the financial health of others as well. No ambiguity. "You need *meds*." I have to be definitive in my own practice of money management.

2. For young people, young women and men: *Vive la différence.* We *are* different. I often see parents and children together. As much as society may want to lump us all together, in the whole spectrum of human nature, it's not that way in reality. Trumpet the differences and admit they exist. I've developed a sense I call, "reading the room." Essentially knowing your characters, hostility, the fears, the hoping for solutions. Body language, which is why I need to see people *in person.*

3. Medical school doesn't teach you to read and respond to human nature. But reading literature and history can help you read a room. I believe that my musical background helps as well. You think about the universe and universal truths if you immerse yourself in music as a profession or as a hobby. You can certainly tell a lot about people's reactions when you tell them that you're an expert on the euphonium. You make yourself a human being to the patient. Then they can trust you more.

4. Be a good listener and emotionally available. I'm an optimist and I never use negativity with my patients. All the taboos are my specialty: eating disorders, sexual issues, menstrual problems, "my folks don't understand me." Eating problems go way back in history. In various religions, women would starve themselves to show obedience to God. Child abuse has also been around for centuries. I tell the patients that they can do what they want. But I give them honesty, including what they don't want to hear. I'll give them

options. I'll say, "I don't take responsibility." It's much better that they make their own decisions. But, I'm their friend. I help them make the tough ones. By the way, grandparents can really make an enormous difference. Because they can offer unconditional love without an agenda.

Most of the time people say, "What?" If you personalize your comments about yourself it's amazing how it opens up the patient for telling *you* their inner truths. You show me, and I'll show you. We're in this process together.

BE CLEAR, DIRECT AND MATERNALISTIC.

35 | LYDIA GOES ON ABOUT 'LIFE IN THE FUTURE'

When the world is at a crossroads, you'd better think about reinventing yourself, no matter what your age. Every corner of society will change post-COVID-19, and healthcare will be at the top of the list. I've learned so much from Dr. Lydia, I wanted our discussion to continue. I came away wishing I was still a teenager and having Lydia for wisdom about many things.

She says: "I anticipate/hope that tech-facilitated care will continue to expand. During the pandemic, not only did we have to see patients via telehealth, but we had to provide education to them and communicate with them in creative ways. In behavioral health care, that meant:

- nutritionist reviews, using an app in treatment of patients with an eating disorder—patient logs her caloric intake and the nutritionist reviews it on a dashboard

- therapists text messaging with clients and recommending apps, websites, online support groups and therapy
- program coordinators, case managers, and mental health professionals sending resources to families via the hospital patient portal
- expanding our library of digital resources
- patients sending forms, photos and videos related to their care via the patient portal

Lydia goes on, "In my research, my team and I made virtual the in-person counseling portion of an intervention to reduce risk of unplanned pregnancy and sexually transmitted infections in young women with depression. The counseling is still done live and still has interactive activities, information, education, skills-building, etc., but it is by video conferencing and website. This intervention also includes an app—participants complete surveys online and receive messages multiple times a day for four weeks. In earlier studies, participants said they felt connected to the counselor and cared for, even though the app is all pre-programmed and not a conversation with a live person. I am working on two other projects both of which involve adolescent patients, completing questionnaires online and the results being available to their primary care clinicians to discuss in their annual check up."

The pandemic has created a mental health epidemic that threatens to overwhelm conventional hospital care. Lydia has guided me, in my amateur involvement with advice to young people, because of the books for them I've written over the last decade. Her advice for fathers who can show anger about eating disorders is to, "Listen and say 'I hear you.' Be that good listener and emotionally available and always let them know that you're coming from a total position of love for them. Of course, it's hard. But it will mean so much to your child if you show them that strength."

She coninues, "But I believe in the power of being in the same space as someone, of being able to touch them to examine and to comfort. I don't want virtual care to supplant in-person care, but rather *augment* it. Tech provides more tools for our tool kit. Wouldn't it be cool if every patient could receive care in a manner customized to their needs and their challenges? I saw a new patient recently who had a substantial medical history. I needed to reconnect her with psychiatric care. On the day of her appointment, her car broke down and she called to reschedule. Instead of canceling her appointment on that day, I switched it to virtual and was able to use the time to get through her history, some of the exam, and, importantly, start a trial of treatment. We then had an in-person visit to follow up on the treatment and to complete the exam. She was SO much better and had gotten a month of her life back. And because we had seen each other's face over Zoom, she got to have a comfortable, familiar visit in person, despite masks and my face shield.

"I also believe in the power of the relationship. One of my most memorable patients was a young woman with a horrific history of childhood sexual trauma who struggled with psychiatric disorders that frequently left her in despair. She was also smart and funny and a prolific writer and poet. Her mother had a psychiatric illness herself and was not always available to my patient in the ways that she needed. I saw this patient often and during the course of our relationship, I became a powerful maternal figure. That transference can be positive—or not so much—and needs to be handled delicately. I believed that with compassionate treatment and development and time, she would heal and find happiness. It was my great privilege to attend her college graduation. She aged out of my practice, but for a long time she would get in touch about once a year to tell me about her life. She went on to graduate school and became a mental health professional."

Lydia laughs easily. No school can teach you to understand human nature and to appreciate what Joni Mitchell sang, "I look at life from both sides now."

"One sidebar to the coronavirus," she tells me, "is that applications to medical schools have skyrocketed. Young people today, one really good thing, they want to help others. But the epidemic of problems for many kids include a high percentage of disadvantaged children in this country who haven't even logged on to classes. So many don't have computers or Wi-Fi. I see patients who are dropping out of school completely. In Massachusetts, by law, you do not have to go to school after 16 years old. It's heartbreaking."

Lydia lists her favorite lessons:

1. "In showing warmth to the patient, you build trust and they start healing themselves, partly because they care what I think of them.

2. "The pandemic has added tools to our treatments. It's forced us to adapt. For instance, virtual visits, like Zoom and FaceTime, have been a way to see people *without* masks, and for them, in isolation, can have a connection to someone who cares about them.

3. "Office visits tend to be very sterile. With video, I can see how people live in their homes, I can see their pets. I can sense the order and the chaos. Which you can never tell from office visits. Virtual is not for every patient. But it certainly allows flexibility and ease of entry. It is more natural in certain ways, not to be in institutional settings.

"But the virtual model is here to stay."

IT'S AS OLD AS TIME. SHOW WARMTH
TO THE PATIENT.

36 | THE SICILIAN

I've always thought that street smarts trumped genius every time with our day-to-day life problems.

Thirty-two years ago, a young woman came into my life, applying for a job as an assistant in my money management business. She had worked as business manager in a hair salon and concierge in an apartment building notorious for its contentious, difficult owners. My business is really a family office, advising hundreds of clients around the world about money management and planning of all kinds for the future. It's a people business and the job description said, "A patient person who is compassionate, with a sense of humor and is cool under pressure." Bridget said to me, "I'm good at all that stuff. What are the benefits?" That almost ended it right there; it was as if she were interviewing *me*. But I let it roll on and ended up thinking that I wanted someone really strong, who was an independent thinker. Bridget was my chief lieutenant for all those 32 years. I fought with her more than I ever fought with my wife. But I think it was good for both of us.

Bridget grew up in New Jersey and lived in a two-family house with her parents and brother. Her grandparents lived downstairs. The family and extended family was huge. There was a pecking order. Age and authority were recognized and observed. In the summers, perhaps 125 people rented cottages on the Jersey Shore. All Bridget's family. Sicily was their roots and everything was according to the culture brought from the old country to America, no dissenters. "My eyes were out on sticks, taking it all in," Bridget told me. "Magical with all the uncles and aunts and the cousins. Boisterous and passionate. But there was order." Bridget said, "One time my grandmother was overwhelmed with pigeons flocking to our house, dumping all over the place. She called one of her brothers high up the family food chain, to do something. The next day, a car pulls up and four of the male cousins got out with BB guns. They must've killed 30 pigeons. Then they got into the car and sped away. No flocks of pigeons came back to the house anymore."

Protocol was essential for order. "Funerals were special occasions," Bridget also told me. "One occasion I saw big fistfights in the parking lot when the cars were lining up to go to the churchyard after the service. Serious fights. Because several cars in the family got in the wrong order, jumping ahead of family members who were more important. Jumping the line had consequences."

Bridget remained cool under pressure ... A client had suddenly died on vacation in Spain, an elderly woman. Her family was hysterical. Bridget got the woman's American Express card number, called them and posed as the woman's daughter and got the body airlifted back to the US. "I lied through my teeth," she said.

This is what I call "adding value to the client." When a married client of ours got divorced, I was sure that one of them would leave our practice. Bridget, without anyone telling her to do this, separately went to visit the estranged husband and wife. She convinced them that they should both stay with us and cited the reasons, especially that we would give equal weight and attention to them and service on into the sunset. She went to dinner with both of them, separately, and made a real, lasting friendship with the wife. None of this was in her job description. This is just one example of adding value.

Bridget retired just before COVID-19 hit, ready to travel and see places on her wish list she never thought she'd get to see. Sad for both of us, particularly me, because I don't believe in retirement ... too insecure to step off the merry-go-round.

Several of her lessons to me have resonated through the decades. Some of them classic Sicilian:

1. If we're in the investment business, or advertising, practicing law or medicine or plumbing ... clients and patients leave us, for many reasons, deserved and undeserved. Every time a client left, Bridget would say, "He, or she, is dead to me." I heard that phrase long before Tony Soprano said the line on the HBO series. "Be passionate about what you do," she said. "Sooner or later you'll be really glad you've dared to be passionate."

2. Bridget had never traveled abroad when I met her. But we had several clients who she took care of who didn't know each other, but frequently visited Paris. One was a man from the Midwest who ran a think tank, specializing in defense, and who was a Republican. The other clients were a couple, highly educated, and politically involved, who were liberal Democrats. Bridget found out that all the clients were going to be in Paris at the same time. Bridget booked a trip to be there when they all arrived. She introduced them to each other. They all went to dinner, with the clients treating Bridget. For parts of that week they took turns showing Bridget the sights and educating her in

all things French. All of them became fast friends on that trip, despite their political differences. Because of Bridget, her love for new adventures, and taking care of people.

The rollout of vaccines was a real challenge in Massachusetts. The website instructions a logistical nightmare, people spending hours on the phone and online trying to make appointments. None of my doctors had any idea when they would get vaccines to dispense. I heard one word from all of them: "Frustration."

One Sunday morning in February 2021, Bridget called me, all excited. "One of my girlfriends had her first shot at some little clinic in the Theater District. I called for you and made you an appointment tomorrow at 3:30." No man I knew had the tenacity to work the system the way she did. The clinic was about a 12-minute walk from my house. I would have been "up the creek without a paddle" if Bridget hadn't gone that extra mile for me. When my wife died in 2011, she and my daughter, Amanda, tag-teamed in every possible way to make sure that I was organized and prepared for the challenges of my new life.

Bridget and I were partners in so many ways. The best relationships are mutually beneficial, filling in the blank spots for the other person. When she retired, she was a millionaire. And we did it in the stock market.

"We can all do this," she told me, "if we take the long view. Buy the best companies slowly and add to them in scary times."

She never waited for life to come to her. She went out there and jumped into it with gusto. La Bella Vita!

YOU ARE LUCKY IF YOU HAVE A SICILIAN IN YOUR LIFE.

37 | THE EDITOR: YOU ALL NEED IS A YOUNG NEW YORK WOMAN ON YOUR TEAM

Vanna Le grew up in San Francisco and early on had dreams of multiple careers in medicine, fashion, journalism. Her brain, always on fire.

I love hearing stories of people's childhood. It reveals so much about what they become as adults. Vanna entered an essay contest in the sixth grade. The theme was "Dare to Dream." She had seen pictures of concentration camps in WWII, which horrified her. They made her angry. She wrote about world peace and and won a $25,000 scholarship for her school. She also got to pick six friends to all go on a trip to New York with her. They were given Apple computers. "This may sound odd," she said, "but I wanted the girls to take the trip seriously. Not treat it as a lark." She told one of the chosen few that she couldn't go. Vanna didn't think this this classmate took it seriously enough. Difficult to make decisions like this when one was so young. You don't want to risk losing a friend who might gossip about you when you're a teenager. But Vanna wasn't a dilettante. She took her mission seriously.

Vanna's not afraid of change. After college in California, she moved east. During her time in Manhattan, she's had a lot of jobs, interning at the *New Yorker*, working at *Vogue* and the *Huffington Post*, associate editor at *Forbes*. Earlier she was an assistant to the Olson twins in Los Angeles, making sure clothes were folded and glass jars were full of cigarettes. "Of course," she told me, "a lot of my education in New York was mostly like *The Devil Wears Prada*. My experience toughened me up to the reality of many rich and successful people. They have monster insecurities and tend to treat underlings like non-humans. They also seem, in spades, to reflect the worst of human behavior. They suck up and bully down. Particularly women in fashion ... mean, mean girls." Now she's in charge of contributors to CNBC's daily melange of business news and life lessons. She reached out to me and asked if I'd be a contributor to their website. Vanna's become my digital penpal, perhaps we'll never meet in person.

I've never had a good friend in my life who I've never met. But the pandemic changed all that. I've never searched for relationships online. I've never even been on a blind date in my life. Except once when my family wanted me to meet a Seagram's liquor heiress, at the time one of the wealthiest families in the world. Picking her up, I got a flat tire on my Volkswagen Bug. It went down from there. Never let your parents fix you up.

Years ago my favorite aunt was not shy with her advice. "Be curious. You'd better have your eyes out on sticks in your life. You never know who can teach you lessons." When my generation got out of college, many of us considered our education lacking if we didn't have a New York experience. The city was a Mecca you had to have lived in, no matter how briefly.

Vanna came to New York like an immigrant. She had $800 and a backpack with some clothes. "I majored in fashion and design in college, I got to New York. Rang the bell at the apartment of my only friend in the city and slept on his couch. When I started at the *New Yorker* I was a gofer really. I was afraid to talk to anyone. They all seemed brilliant to me. But brilliance doesn't mean you're kind or compassionate."

As I write this, I've been working for Vanna for about six months. She's in charge of contributors to the website of CNBC, the business channel. I've been doing what I call "mood pieces" for her, little essays about how to get ahead in life using "street smarts." Vanna is my editor. She's a millennial. If we're curious about life today in America, you need to have people in that generation in your life who are *not* family. You need fresh eyes on that generation. Family are too close and personal. Too much love. Too much guilt.

She's become my eyes and ears into the younger generations in New York City. As a money manager, part of the job is identifying trends before they really explode; and New York is the capital of the world in so many ways that define culture.

When I met Vanna, via email, she told me, "I just bought my first apartment, my little window on the world. I sit and watch the people in the street and try to imagine who they are and what they do. Sometimes I sit outside the entrance with the doorman, imagining the lives of the people passing by."

Vanna is an editor who knows what she wants from her contributors: money managers, psychologists, economists, college professors, all feeding the need for content that is informative and even entertaining,

"Tell me about your typical day," I asked her.

"I get up about 6:30 and spend an hour stretching and doing breathing exercises that can change your life." I'm a sucker for anyone who says they can change my life.

———

Vanna comes from a generation immersed in healthy lifestyles, diet and exercise. Why wouldn't I want to go for the fountain of youth channelled through Vanna? Here's her breathing routine:

1. Sit cross-legged and place both hands on thighs. Slowly breathe in through the nose for five seconds. Slowly breathe out for five seconds. This is how you tell your body, "wake up, the day has begun."

2. Next is nostril breathing. More fun than it sounds—and a wonderful way to balance your energy. Use the right thumb to plug your right nostril, breathe in through the left. Then plug your left nostril with your index finger, breathe out through the right. Keep alternating five times on each side.

3. In yoga, we call this next one "Breath of Fire," and it releases tension and negative energy.

    To start: do a quick, forceful inhale through your nostrils into your lungs ... of medium intensity, but not overexerting yourself. Without pausing, exhale with an equally matched level of force as your inhale. Be sure the exhale is the same length and depth as the inhale. Repeat.

    Continue these dynamic inhales and exhales without pausing. The inhales should seamlessly merge into the exhales, and vice versa. Once you're comfortable and have gotten into the rhythm of the flow, bring your attention to your core stomach muscles, and use it to power the breath. Do this for 30 seconds.

4. To end the breathing practice, draw in a long and deep inhale and slowly release your hands down by your side. As your breath becomes neutral, set an intention to clear any leftover or blocked energy around you.

"You don't need painkillers," continues Vanna. "The breathing relaxes me. You need to relax somehow to survive in New York.

In my early days, I was folding $500 tee shirts for the Olsens and being a gofer; the powerful women in fashion needed their gofers. At *Vogue*, I'd do all the Christmas shopping for my boss. I'd pick up her dry cleaning, steam clothes for a photo shoot. I got scoliosis from carrying seven baked hams for 20 blocks, all for my boss, for presents. The power women in New York are killers. But," Vanna says, "'sucking it up' for these women taught me a great lesson. You have to prep yourself, to emotionally expect to *fail*. It's not ultimately about skills in this town. It's about mental toughness."

The people I learn most from seem to have contrasting approaches to life, people who are always surprising to me, like a woman dermatologist who is also a golf champion who seems to be happier on a golf course than checking for melanoma. In other words, often people's secret lives can mean more than where they earn their livelihoods.

If you want a quick character study of people, two simple questions can tell you volumes about people ... "What's your all-time favorite book?" and "What's your all time favorite movie?"

Of course, I asked Vanna. She didn't skip a beat. "Dickens' *Great Expectations*." This is why I have always, since I grew an adult brain, wanted to have smart New York women in my life.

I loved *Great Expectations* as well; my favorite movie version starred Jean Simmons. I fell in love with Jean Simmons. The answers to these book and movie questions reveal so much about the person. The heroine in *Great Expectations* is Estella, orphaned, and then raised by Miss Havisham, who was jilted on her wedding day. She brought up Estella to "break their hearts," meaning the heart of any man courting her.

Nothing is easy for this smart New York woman. I have been taught lessons before Vanna, by New York women from the time I was in my early twenties. They were all distinguished, even famous women of New York, from fields as diverse as advertising, retail, education and television. *All* of them were/are stand-alones, fiercely independent, smart, taking no prisoners, although often masking the intensity with common sense and humor. The humor that allows for understanding life's absurdities.

Vanna belongs to the cadre of women I know who have carved out special niches for themselves in varied professions. But they've all shared an intense resilience, which Vanna notes is the most important quality in making it in New York. This hasn't changed over the decades.

My children's generation will inherit more money than any generation in history. But that generation, as I view that landscape, will blow it, spend it, ratchet it down, no matter how much was showered upon them. It's *Vanna's* generation and younger who will reap the whirlwind. Her resilience to "do it herself," and prosper ultimately in any setting, is the lesson I want all young people to know. Resilience and hard work. Sounds boring, right? But her generation better have the work ethic or else they will suffer.

Every day, Vanna juggles multiple contributors to CNBC's daily feed. She finds the talent, suggests topics, edits the submissions, and feeds it into the website. It's creative and exhausting and the information beast needs to be fed every day.

"How do you relax?"

"I exercise each morning, as I said. I cook. I walk my dog in the park. I throw pots. I read. I watch people from my window and pretend I'm in their lives. My favorite place in my favorite museum, the MOMA, is the gallery that shows Salvador Dali. I love his audacity, his mischievousness, his take on what flaws exist in life. His color. When I'm down, I go visit Dali."

I hope to keep writing for Vanna and hearing her take on things. I told her how much I notice women being more in charge of everything.

"I can tell you," she says, "most of the men I know seem to be having their midlife crisis in their thirties. And most of my younger colleagues don't want to go back to the office. To me the office is where you grow, where you really get graduate school. The office."

If Vanna is really Estella, it's too late for anyone to break my heart. But I'm rooting for her mental toughness to make sure that, sooner or later … she wins.

IT TAKES RESILIENCE, MORE THAN ANYTHING ELSE, TO MAKE IT IN NEW YORK.

38 | GRACE UNDER PRESSURE

Yvonne was working as a temp and came into our office to fill-in for a sales assistant on vacation. She worked for a real character in our office. He often came to work wearing tennis shorts, with mismatched socks, one red, one green ... like port and starboard. But it was totally random, whatever he grabbed when he woke up. He was also a slob, tossing lunch containers, contents half-eaten underneath his desk. Yvonne would clean up his mess.

One day, Yvonne came to work early. She went into the man's office knowing she'd have to clean up, and saw legs sticking out from under the desk. She screamed. I would have screamed. She thought he was dead. The man's wife had delivered a baby at dawn that day. He had been at the hospital and had left mother and babe to rest. He came in about 6 a.m., exhausted, and lay down under his desk, legs sticking out ... and crashed. I had watched Yvonne be unflappable, under a difficult situation and offered her a permanent job. She told me about her job experience and how she had been an international courier, delivering documents all over Europe. That job sounded very mysterious, and the romantic in me fantasized that she had been a secret agent, or a "hit woman" for the CIA. When I'd tell her what I guessed about her career, she'd just give me a Mona Lisa smile and brush my comments aside. We've worked together for over 30 years and she still seems to be somewhat of a mystery to me, a quite private, elegant woman, who glides through market ups and downs never getting excited or frazzled.

She's taught me many things over the years. Aside from the investment world during the days, Yvonne has been my editorial assistant at her home, typing from my yellow legal pad hen-scratchings and bringing me hard copy later. Editing as well, returning her pages with a second copy marked, "My 2 Cents" Most of the time I defer to her discerning eye, both of us working both sides of the brain, the creative and the practical.

Yvonne has probably typed hundred of thousands of words for me, many fragments of books that never got to print, hundreds of magazine articles, and columns for media as diverse as *The Atlantic* magazine, the *Boston Globe*, and CNBC, often meeting frantic deadlines. Me being the frantic one. She being the calm in the storm. Yvonne grew up on Cape Cod, with five brothers, which may explain her demeanor. Somehow she seemed born to be on an even keel ... unflappable.

Every day she arrived to work as if she labored for *Vogue* or *Mademoiselle*, impeccably groomed. Boston, traditionally, had been a city that has never really paid attention to dress. The men in the financial world and the male lawyers, all in the same uniform, suits and vests and ties, many on the Yankee side, wearing the smart, English hand-me-downs from fathers and grandfathers. The women dressed in what my daughter would call "whatevah." Yvonne wore something smashing every day. Once she said to me, "I think of Paris when I pick outfits and imagine that I'm there. I also love the glamour of the old movies, Kate Hepburn, Bette Davis. I only really stay in this job because of *your* creative life, not the investment side. I do love the stock market, but the fantasy side of your life keeps me around."

Yvonne has hung around for more than 32 years, and by the time you read this, she will have retired from her daily investment life, and the commute by boat to Boston.

Here's what I've learned from Yvonne in the last three decades:

1. I work in the money business. But I always knew I needed to keep a creative side going, so that I wouldn't be one dimensional. When I was a little girl, I'd knock on my dad's office door. He was a doctor. He'd give me a pad of paper and pencils and I'd sit on his office steps and draw. I inherited my mother's paint box. I'm drawn to all things artistic, and I enjoy the painting journey.

2. I'm a voracious reader as well. There was a library down our street. I'd walk there as a child and check out armloads of books. My Mom was a great word game enthusiast, and a stickler for grammar. I think I'm a self-taught editor because of that.

3. I was never interested in money really, and I always thought I'd work in a lawyer's office with my editing skills. But I stayed in the investment world with John Spooner, who has such a love for humanity that I wanted to be along for the ride. I think our money management team helps to make the world a better place.

"If you're in a happy work situation," continued Yvonne. "You can also learn new skills. I've learned to invest in areas where I use the products or services. It's the Peter Lynch theory of buying what you know. I've been a Portfolio Associate for my entire career, but in the graduate school of real life, I've actually invested to the point where my portfolio has allowed me to retire comfortably with a nest egg I never thought I'd have. You can do it too if you learn these lessons. Renoir had a saying that he was like 'the cork in the river,' you never know what life holds for you downstream."

Yvonne is a millionaire. She did it in the stock market.

OPEN YOUR EYES TO NEW WAYS OF LOOKING AT THE WORLD.

39 | GETTING TO YES: VIVIAN SPIRO

Fund raising is generally a well-paid profession and a hard one. Hard because it never stops. If you work in the field for a non-profit or a private school or college and you bring in a major gift of seven figures, everyone cheers and congratulates you. Then, the next day, your boss will say, "What have you done for me lately?" In my experience, the people with the gift of "getting to yes" are *not* on staff. They're on the board of their organizations, and often "the Chair." They're the real fund raisers.

I can think of three people in my city who have this talent. One of them is Vivian Spiro, who took a part of the Boston Public Library and, from a standing start, built the Associates of the Public Library into a force.

The annual gala she spearheaded, called Literary Lights, honors New England's most accomplished writers. I've been to hundreds of galas in various cities, and the Literary Lights benefit is almost the only one people are thrilled to attend. Because everyone who comes loves books and meeting the honorees who all sit at tables with the paying guests. More than 700 people turn out in formal dress to pass the salt to writers like the late David McCullough, Doris Kearns Goodwin, Henry Louis Gates or Lydia Diamond. Most people, if they're honest, tend to say about these annual fund raisers, "Please, can't I just send a check and not actually go?" But never when Vivian has gotten you there. Almost all of those 700 people come to honor her passion, dedication and the brilliance of her remarks as she welcomes everyone from the dais. Her introductions are little gems, teeing up the honorees.

Every year from the time she became involved, she gave the opening address. Robert Parker, the great mystery writer who created the *Spenser* series told me, "I'd go just to listen to Vivian, not those other stiffs." He was irreverent. But he nailed it. They come for Vivian.

So few people I've known in my life have had this ability to get people to say "yes." Here's what Vivian has told me. "It's pretty simple. You have to convey to people that you care passionately about the cause and that you put your own energy and a lot of time and your own money into what you care for. You also have to make the case that you're the person prospecting and that you should care about it as well. Also *why* you should care.

"The other element to get people to say 'yes' is that you have something that other people *want,* selfishly that you'll be seen with a certain 'in crowd.'"

In Vivian's case, she and her husband, Lionel, are what is these days called "influencers." They are cultural leaders. They entertain, and you want to be at their parties or dinners and you want to be seen about town with them. There's a relatively new acronym going around these days: FOMO ... "fear of missing out." You want to be "in" with that "in crowd," a natural tendency. It's human nature. Because people want this acceptance, they will contribute time and money to Vivian's tenacity and her caring about causes, and want to join her posse.

It can be easy to say "no" to the requests from so many people in our lives, for many reasons …

But there are some people we cannot resist.

LEARN THE LESSONS OF PEOPLE WHO GET YOU TO SAY "YES."

40 | THE MARKETER

It's so rare that any of us ever know someone who may be the best at what they do of anyone in the country. I think I know one. She is Shelly Lazarus, retired now as the CEO of Ogilvy & Mather in New York, one of America's premier advertising agencies.

Shelly went to Smith College. She majored in government and psychology, strictly by accident. A friend convinced her to take a three-hour course with her, really to keep her friend company. Luck does play a role in life. But you have to be "out there" to take advantage when luck pops in. "It was a three-hour program," Shelly told me, "on advertising and marketing. I could have stayed all day it was so exciting to me. I never thought there was any strategy to ads. I was so excited by this that I applied for a job with J. Walter Thompson. The only job available for women, I was told, was in typing ... a secretary."

My first novel was published in 1967. I remember those days. It was *The Pheasant-lined Vest of Charlie Freeman*, really the *Catcher in the Rye* of Wall Street. There were virtually no women editors at the time. The only jobs really in publishing for women were as secretaries. Today, women dominate publishing, at every level. Women are 80% of the book buyers in America.

Shelly went on. "Thompson told me to go get an MBA. If you got an MBA, they can't make you type. Honestly, I didn't even know what an MBA *was*."

But she took Thompson at their word and got her MBA at Columbia in 15 months. "Business school was *hard*," she said, "but Smith taught me a crucial thing. They taught me to *write*." Shelly told me that she was only one of four women out of 300 students at Columbia B-School. "I think I had an obsession," she said. "I just didn't want to *type*.

"My first job was the Maxwell House Coffee account. I was an intern and also the first woman there. This was during the Vietnam War." Again, luck played a role. Shelly said, "I had two bosses. They were both in the Army Reserve and they *both* got called back into active duty service. I took over the account. I learned and I left and went to work for Clairol. There was *one* woman there. Bristol Myers owned Clairol. I loved it for two years, when a headhunter called. They told me that Ogilvy & Mather was looking for a woman who knew *hair*. Well, that would be me. I joined Ogilvy and Mather and never looked back."

At Ogilvy, Shelly became only the second woman ever to be chosen for account management. "Back when I was at General Foods I had a woman friend who was five months pregnant but hadn't told the company," Shelly told me. "When it became apparent what was happening, she wasn't allowed into the building. This was in the 1970s. Outrageous. I was determined to make clients accept women."

I asked Shelly if she had strong women friendships, close ties with women outside of work who were in constant touch.

"You know," she said, "this may sound strange, but I had so much interaction every day, that I had *no* time for social life outside of Ogilvy with women friends. But I seemed to be a natural at getting along with men. I never wanted to be a cheerleader in high school. I was editor of the paper. Never a loner but I do need alone time to think … I don't like to share, but my best friends growing up were boys … my buddies. I like to keep it interesting. And *luck* does play a role, even in health issues. One of my little boyfriends gave me a cigarette to try when I was eight. I got sick and never smoked again because of the experience. Total dumb luck."

In her early days at Ogilvy, Shelly was working on a new product with the team. They had a meeting in Rye, New York, to energize and inform their sales force. When they got there the client was in a froth because ad posters were not up on the wall. One of her team said, "I went to Harvard Business School. I'm not going to put up the posters." Shelly said, "I went to Columbia Business School. I'm going to climb on chairs and hang the posters." She took off her heels and did it. "We do what we have to do. Regardless," Shelly says. "Never be too good to do the job."

Shelly came into my life originally as a client. She and her husband George, a noted New York pediatrician, had an escape home in the Berkshires. A woman financial advisor in the firm where I worked, also had a home nearby, loving the music in the summers at Tanglewood. That friend, Barbara Lee, managed money for Shelly and George. In her early forties, Barbara was diagnosed with cancer. She suggested that if her disease forced her to leave her business, that Shelly reach out to me. The very sad accidents of life brought the Lazarus family to me in the late 1990s.

Shelly's ability to make friends with men launched her at Ogilvy. It was *Mad Men* time. But they let her into the club. Her first real break came with American Express, an Ogilvy client. She was asked to be on a task force to develop a five-year strategic plan. "I was the only woman included and I was secretly terrified," she told me. "They gave me one topic to explore: *How do we enter Japan?* I knew nothing about Japan. But I forced myself to reach into my list of friends and classmates, friends of friends, teachers. I realized that I didn't know anything about Japan. But I found five smart people who *did*. They knew the answers and gave me the confidence to take us into Japan. I had my new theory that has served me well throughout my career: You didn't have to have the answers. You just need to find the five people who *did* have the answers."

Shelly's masterstroke came because of her work as a managing supervisor on Ogilvy's American Express account. Her team's work was so successful and AMEX was growing so fast that she gained the admiration and trust of the CEO, Lou Gerstner. I keep writing about the influence of luck in life. But I also hammer on the second part of this: you have to be *out there* to take advantage of luck when it arrives. Lou Gerstner left AMEX to take the CEO role at IBM. At the time, IBM was having problems and desperately needed to refresh the brand. They also had 72 separate ad agencies, spread all over the world. Not a good model for turning a classic company around. Gerstner trusted Shelly through the prior relationship that produced results. *All* of IBM's business came to Ogilvy and Shelly Lazarus. Shelly's mandate was to "fix the brand" for that iconic company. The best way to fix the brand was to use one agency and work with people Gerstner had trusted for many years, particularly Shelly Lazarus. Shelly had another friend already at IBM, Abby Kohnstamm. They became the secret to focusing the new IBM in their marketing. "We showed everyone the traditional pattern of white men was just plain *wrong*. It wasn't about quotas. It was about getting the right talent on board in key positions."

Shelly, over our 25-year relationship, has taught me a lot about what makes true leadership. I've always felt a bit intimidated by her. She's moved in the highest circles on both corporate and nonprofit boards, from GE and Merck, to Blackstone, Columbia Business School, Smith College, and FINRA, the securities industry watch dog. She doesn't suffer fools. But this is what produces results: She makes people perform better than they knew they could. She gets the people who work for her to "play up." They sense that she expects excellence. I want to perform for *her* and not let her down. What a quality.

Here are snippets of Shelly's wisdom:

1. Because I've always have had friendships with men, they tend to be honest with me, particularly when I was growing up in the advertising business where there were very few women in power positions. If you were in these positions as a woman you had to really pour yourself into work. Having men tell me things they wouldn't really say to women helped so much when I was young. One special man, a real pro, gave me good advice. He said, "Don't be a pain in the ass around the house."

   If I didn't have the ability to have men friendships, no one would have given me this lesson. They wanted me to succeed.

2. Marketing: If you define marketing as seeing the world outside in, you'll never really succeed. You have to see the world from the *inside out*. You start with the *end-user*. You have to see the world through the user's eyes, the consumer's eyes. That's how you sell a product ... or anything, really. In the corporate world, I was never surprised by cluelessness. I told one CEO, "I think like a customer. Have you ever tried calling your company's main number?" He hadn't. When he did, in my presence, he slammed the phone down and got red in the face. If it was confusing to *him*, what about the clients? Another example. Everyone passes through a lobby if your companies name is on the building. I had lunch one time with the CEO of Arthur Andersen, the giant auditing firm. "What does your lobby say about you?" I asked him. "There's a coffee table with three years of accounting magazines on it. You're so much

more than accounting. Sit in your own reception area. Go to your website. Is *this* what you want people to think about you? It's your front door." Shelly goes on. "If it's *your* building, visitors' first impression involves the parking guys. They take your car. They're your ambassadors. Train them to be helpful, friendly and gracious. This will make all visitors impressed with the way you run you operations before they even get on an elevator."

3. Women have empathy in how they view the world. In marketing we have the advantage. I love the fact that people are so irrational. For instance, we did the campaigns for Unilever, for Dove soap. What is beauty? We did a survey for them about H and B, health and beauty. One of the things we asked was, "Do you think you're beautiful?" Only six percent answered "yes." This struck a nerve. We launched a campaign focused on the unique quality of Dove. It wasn't soap. It was not a drier of skin, it was cold cream. Perfect for babies. Perfect for beautiful *you*. Dove went beyond soap. It started a conversation about *beauty*. That's what we were selling: Dove is so much more than soap ... It's your path to something much greater. This is what great advertising is supposed to do.

4. Even if you're a certain kind of a loner, needing to step back and consider what the challenges are, if you're lucky you have a partner. At the end of every day, it's a blessing to have someone who does something entirely different from what you do. My husband George is a doctor, a pediatrician. He thinks it's absurd to get worked up over an *ad*, compared to what he deals with. George has perspective. If you choose a partner in life, and you've always chosen independent roads

for yourself ... choose a partner who has nothing to do with your professional life. It really helps.

5. People love lists, the "top ten" of this or that, books, songs, baseball players, movies, actors, etc. I was on the list of most powerful women in the world, for instance. One list had me more powerful than the Queen of England. How absurd. That's when, to someone who called wanting to put me on a list, I said, "No, thanks." Plus, to make it interesting, the people who make up lists have to change the lists every year. Lists are arbitrary and mostly bogus. More powerful than the Queen? Don't be sucked into the absurd.

6. You have to find what you love in life and pursue it. I didn't think of my career as work. It was always inherently interesting. The corporate world is trying to mold people. To really succeed, *be who you are.* To young women: Don't play a role all day; find a place in your own skin to thrive. Have faith in what you think. It's exhausting to be put in some kind of box made up by corporate culture. Break out of the box.

I asked Shelly, as I've asked all of the women in this book, "What is your all-time favorite movie, and your all-time favorite book?" Without hesitation, she said, "*Rebecca* is my favorite movie and *Pride and Prejudice,* my all-time favorite book."

SEE THE WORLD THROUGH THE CONSUMER'S EYES.

41 | CONCERNING THE CABLE GUY AND CONNECTIVITY

My friend Margaret believes that "all life is relationships." She has an uncanny ability to remember the name of everyone she meets *and* the names of their children and grandchildren. She also asks almost everyone with whom she interacts about themselves: auto mechanics, waiters, nail salon workers, teachers, police, snowplow drivers. This is not a ploy. She honestly is curious about how people live their lives. But by naturally doing this, she binds people to her.

Almost all of us have problems with our communication devices: TVs, phones, computers, you name it. Everyday I get up in the morning and the first thing I say is, "Is *anything* easy?" It's not.

Recently, Margaret called me, all excited. "I hit the jackpot today," she said. "In front of my supermarket, there's an Xfinity truck parked. The driver is sitting at the wheel, eating a sandwich, window rolled down. I went right over to him. 'Hi,' I said, 'this is your lucky day because you can solve a hundred problems for me.'"

Hyperbole gets people's attention. By the time Margaret finished her conversation with the Xfinity man, she had gotten from him, his personal phone number to troubleshoot whatever she needed, the inside scoop on how to lower your cable/phone costs by 20%, and his eternal devotion. She had his name and the names of his kids committed to memory.

"If you ever see a parked Xfinity truck, go up and introduce yourself to the driver," she told me. "It can make your life much easier, and a lot better."

Sometimes, the shorter the story that teaches a lesson, the more it sinks in.

MAKE EVERYTHING PERSONAL.

42 | UNEXPECTED CONSEQUENCES

My sister Susie is a woman full of curiosity about history, stock markets, wine adventures and people. Recently she had a scary bout of double pneumonia, "life-threatening" as it was called by a friend of hers when he informed me by phone. Scary. It had a happy ending thank goodness, with infusion of antibiotics just in time.

Her first day in the hospital after IVs had brought her back from *in extremis*, a doctor took her on a walk around the floor to measure her oxygen levels.

During the walk my sister complimented this quite small local hospital on their service and attention to detail. "This experience has been so really lovely," she said, "I'm wondering, are there some special things you'd like to have here that you're missing?"

The doctor seemed to be taken aback. "Well," he said, "we always have a wish list. We could use a new laboratory facility badly. And a nurse's lounge would be on that list. Thanks for asking."

For the next 24 hours my sister said, "Various doctors came into my room to say hello. And nurses came in with fruit and cookies between meals. One brought in some flowers that weren't sent by anyone I know."

"They thought you were a potential big giver."

"Bingo," my sister said. "It's hysterical. What a great way to get noticed. Pampered. I jumped to the head of the line." She paused and smiled. "I'm going to try this every time I go to a hospital."

"Me too," I said.

EVEN IF PEOPLE "THINK" THEY SMELL THE MONEY ... THEY'LL RESPOND.

43 | HEY JUDE: THE HEALER

My healer was raised as if she were a heroine in a Henry James novel. I've known Jude Wheelock in all of her adult lives and there have been a few. Her stories about growing up remind me of my early readings of fairytales: knights and ladies, witches and dragons.

She grew up in Watertown, upstate New York, and in the summers the family moved to an island in the St. Lawrence River. "A river that flows north," she points out, "like the Nile." Her dad was a major league sportsman of the old school, living like a lord of the high country. He raised Jude as if he was raising a son, teaching her upland shooting and hunting, including shooting from the hip with a shotgun like John Wayne.

For me, it's wonderfully refreshing to spend time with someone interested in things I have absolutely no idea about. Then I think, maybe she's on to something, exploring mind/body solutions to problems.

The greatest compliment I could ever pay to someone is, "You're never boring." I am big on preaching to young people that they should ask their parents about *their* lives growing up and getting the stories about family and their past. They should ask grandparents as well, so the young will learn "who they are and where they came from." Jude is never boring.

You could spend an evening with Jude, listening to her give chapter and verse about both sides of her family going back 100 years or more. The biggest treat is that she'll throw in phrases like, "You know, I'm also descended from Cleopatra … And possibly Joan of Arc." How can you not love the imagery and be drawn into her alluring net?

When you're young as a man, if you meet another young man who seems to be on a mission, you might give him a wide berth, as if he's crazy. If a man meets a woman on a mission, he will very likely find her fascinating.

Years ago Jude got interested in astrology. Friends would tell my wife and me, "I'm going over to Jude's house. She's going to read my palm and read my signs as well. I'm a Virgo and I'm very excited." Many people follow their signs, checking their horoscopes daily, and also the signs of people in their family. The English are obsessed with astrology. I have very smart friends in London who won't plan a vacation unless they consult their astrologer.

People flocked to Jude because people love to have others tell them about themselves. I believe it's a kind of therapy. But reading signs wasn't enough for Jude. Years ago she went to a wedding in Santa Fe for a woman friend, who was a former Boston debutante turned Buddhist in the desert air of New Mexico. This Buddhist bride-to-be, called it off at the last minute. She also convinced Jude to stay in Santa Fe and go to a lecture by a man from Mexico on aromatherapy, applied by the rubbing on of essential oils. Jude, also on that visit, fell in love with a little house that "spoke to her." She called her husband, Morgan, an eminent landscape architect, and said, "Morgie, we're buying a house." She had long since decided to devote her life to helping others, through aromatherapy; and her own unique way of making even casual evenings into a conversation, like a therapy session in the most gentle way possible. It wasn't enough that she was learning ways to make her life more meaningful. She wanted *you* to benefit as well.

"Driving into Santa Fe at the time," she told me, "I couldn't believe the vastness of this country, stretching out before me, the desert, the mountains the sunrise and sunsets. What grew from the ground in the West was amazing. I had to pull over on the side of the road and cry because of the landscape I saw before me. That's why I bought the Santa Fe house. I could ski in the mornings and in the afternoons I could do drawings for a local decorator. We're all searching for our spiritual home, whether we know it or not. I found mine in Santa Fe. My friend who almost married, took me to hear that man from Mexico give a lecture on aromatherapy; curing what ails you, relieving pain and stress with essential oils."

"What are essential oils?" I asked her.

"Well, myrrh, frankincense, grapefruit, black pepper, sandalwood, for example. They come from gum and fruit peel, berries, dried fruit, wood, leaves: the extract of many natural things that have been cures for centuries." She couldn't get a license to mix and sell oils as a cure or balm for anything in the US. So she went to London for two years of classes where she could learn the art. There she rubbed elbows with the Duke of Bedford and Sean Connery, among many others, her stories harkening back to days when "the sun never set on the British Empire." She does make unusual friendships wherever she goes.

When she came back to Boston, equipped with oils from all over the world, friends told her that she could be the next Estée Lauder, that if she packaged and promoted her oils, she'd make a fortune. Here's what she told me, "When I was little, living, as my father used to say, 'in the castle on the hill,' in upstate New York, I had a fantasy life. I made all the clothing for my dolls. I lost myself in the gardens surrounding my house. There weren't really a lot of little friends around in this nature paradise right out of James Fenimore Cooper. So I read and observed and decided at this early age, that I wanted to help other people. I didn't want to go for the gold."

In her London period, she had to study chemistry, philology. "If you mix that with an understanding of human nature, you can go out there and save a lot of people. If you believe in yourself and your skills, you get a kick out of show and tell. I can read your palm, tell your fortune, let you know what are the best colors for your clothing, and mix oils to relieve your arthritis." I just stared at her and said nothing.

"I'm not kidding," she said.

Jude keeps coming back to the sense of *smell*, comparing it to how we savor the universe. I'm usually a bit snarky about matters of cosmic importance—but she's so convincing about her interpretations of life that listening to her "show and tell," I get sucked into the program. I asked her at one point, "Do you only rub the oils on? Taste should be as important as smell, yes?"

So many people are grieving now, in *my* life. And losing someone dear to me, I think, almost weekly. Not to mention the epidemic of loneliness and depression among the young in this country. I have doctor friends at Children's Hospital who tell me, "It *is* an epidemic. And we don't have enough people or the beds to treat the problems we see daily."

"So how do you manage the many people you seem to care for? I asked Jude. "And all just for the joy you take from what you do."

Jude smiled at me. We were chatting at her house.

"Let me show you something." She took me into her office that seemed more like a laboratory you'd imagine alchemists working in, looking to create gold. She opened several large cabinet drawers that revealed hundreds of small bottles, all labeled with the names of essential oils, many of them going back thousands of years to Egyptian tombs.

"So how do you reclaim life from anxiety and depression?" I asked her.

Jude says, "You have to *touch* people. I mean really, laying on of hands. A simple touch connects us. Another key that we neglect or seldom think about, is the sense of smell. Have you ever smelled lilacs, for instance, or fennel, or tennis courts in the summer? Do you know that it takes three dozen rosebuds to make *one drop* of oil? For my creations I use so many smells: Peru balsam, distillation of pine needles. I let my formulas sit. And I talk to them. You know how old these healing methods are? There are 352 references to essential oils in the Bible. Good advice is eternal."

Jude smiled. "You can even *drink* my oils. Almost everyone in America prefers the tactile approach. The French love to drink and taste everything. They'll drink the oils. But really, only the French."

As an example, I questioned her on the use of frankincense in her oils.

"Why do you think the Wise Men brought frankincense and myrrh to Bethlehem? she said. "Frankincense is like a glue. It sticks on the side of trees. Shepherds used to notice goats rubbing their faces on these trees, to soak up the smell, knowing that the essence of the oil on the tree would make them feel better, that it would take pain away."

That's what my "healer" spends her life doing, Taking the pain away.

For years, every time I caught a cold, it would end up as a cough that often would go on for weeks. Nothing seemed to work on it. I told Jude about this and within a few days she dropped off a small bottle. "This will help," she said. No hesitation. "It has cinnamon, camphor extract in it, myrtle grain, tea tree. Tea tree smells terrible but the other essences will overcome this and the resulting smell is beyond pleasant. And it heals."

I rubbed it on my neck and chest. I tried, as in Peter Pan, to "think lovely thoughts." And it worked.

Men should pay attention and more to what women know instinctively: the human touch, the smells of spring. Your personal relationships will grow and thrive.

THERE ARE MANY WAYS TO LOOK AT LIFE—
LEARN SOMETHING NEW EVERY DAY.

44 | THE JOURNALIST: ALISON BETHEL

Alison Bethel is an African American journalist. "A journalist all of my life, even as a little girl, when it was only in my imagination." Alison's mother was a huge influence on her life. "She was brilliant intellectually," Alison told me, "but even better, she was street smart. Not shy with her opinions and her advice to me. But boy, she was right."

Alison grew up in Miami, in a very unusual community, Richmond Heights. It was carved out after World War II specifically for African American officers in the armed forces and their families. Not enlisted men of the military. *Only* officers. The thinking was that the officer class would create this unusual community, an elite setting really, that would be a model for minority success, for middle class hard workers. It was.

Life is unfair of course. But sometimes it's unfair in our favor.

Alison was surrounded by smart, successful neighbors with the work ethic. They educated their children to do the same, to go out in the world and succeed.

"We were among the first community that participated in busing. I was in elementary school, taken to a completely white community. It was terrifying to me and to everyone on my bus. The point was to have this lead to desegregation. But we were all segregated in the white school, because we all stayed tight with each other. But the school changed my life.

"In the sixth grade we had 'career day.' It came with a visitor every year who spoke to the kids about their profession. That year, the speaker was Sandra Dibble from the *Miami Herald*. She won a Pulitzer Prize. She blew me away and I came home and told my mother that I wanted to write when I grew up. My experience in the school was different from all my friends, because I had a focus, the student newspaper. I persisted at this. By the ninth grade, I was the editor-in-chief. This was in the 1970s. A Black man was killed in Miami and there were riots. Try going through life when you're terrified in your own community. And it's America." Alison went on. "At the height of the riots, we couldn't get home from school. The white kids could walk home. We were all put in the gym. There was no attempt to mix us. You learn a lot from stuff like this. You never forget it. And you can never understand it unless you've lived through it."

"Do you think things are better today in this fractured society?" Alison smiled a wry smile. "I went to a high school reunion recently. Still: the Black kids sat together. The white kids sat together. They did a video covering the reunion. I was the only African American who made the final cut. It never ends. What does this tell you about things not changing?"

Back when Alison was applying for colleges, her mother chimed in again with practical wisdom. "You should apply to an *all-Black* school," her mom told her. "Think about it. You've spent too much time as 'the only one' in high school and before. It's exhausting being the 'only one.' You should go to Howard. Howard is in DC, our capital. They've got the *Washington Post* and close to the *Baltimore Sun*. Great newspapers." We should all have mothers this street smart.

"So I went to Howard," Alison told me. "My eyes were out on sticks, wonderful, really smart … and everyone my color. They even had sororities on 'The Hilltop.' I learned that there were mean girls everywhere I would go in life. The sororities didn't take me, but I threw myself into writing for the school paper and just missed being editor-in-chief. I had the dream and the itch."

Alison interned every summer. "I worked for Knight Ridder. I worked with Sam Donaldson at NBC News. I didn't get too far there. He thought I asked 'too many questions.' How the hell does one learn? I wanted to know. But the tough lessons gave me grit. I never gave up. I think that's why *The Wizard of Oz* has been one of my favorite movies. Dorothy took everything that was thrown at her, with humor and grace. Two other favorites are Bette Midler's *Beaches*, and, believe it or not, *Gone With the Wind*."

One thing that Alison has taught me, a critical lesson for everyone which she learned the hard way, "cut through the crap." Have a good-sized BS meter, know the real people from the ones mouthing platitudes and wringing their hands about "injustice" without having a clue. But Alison can love Dorothy in Oz and have as her favorite book, *Sweet Pea*, about a young black girl from Mississippi who bathes in a bucket.

Alison Bethel teaches me to "always have a dream … and don't be deterred by anyone." All of we ambitious people have had to plow ahead over the years to achieve what measure of success we've had. Many bumps in the road along the way and many rejections as well, from institutions and from people. I've suffered certain kinds of prejudice as well, always bottling it in and never really discussing it with anyone. But nothing like the obstacles African Americans face very day.

Alison now lives in Washington, DC, and works with a four-year old startup, Report for America, a great idea. They find emerging journalists and plug them into newsrooms around the country to cover local news, areas that are missing coverage everywhere because of the loss of small town and city newspapers.

She is one of those rare people who can be romantic in her sensibilities about books and movies that transport her into other worlds. She also has the practical side that solves problems in a tough real world, not giving into the romantic side when she needs to be strong and resilient.

"Any regrets?" I asked her.

"Well," she said. "I believe in my mission now. Journalism upholds democracy. And we desperately need local news coverage. But I miss the exhilaration of actually writing. You search, search for the first sentence. Then it finally clicks, and you're off with your story. The young kids these days in our profession seem afraid of their own shadows. They need tough love. Life is hard. I've had editors who threw things at me. Bottles. Coffee cups. Stop with the coddling. Get back into the city rooms. Ideas come from being with people. No more 'imposter syndrome' and saying things like 'I'm threatened by the workplace.' Grow some thick skin."

I asked Alison about the future of race relations.

"Well," she said, "I spent several years working in Europe. They face up to the truth there. No attempt to hide fascism. Austria had to be honest about Hitler. Europe cares much more about 'the State' than they do about race. The US pays a lot of lip service to equality. But there's not a lot of action. I have many white friends. Republican friends too. Short term, I'm not optimistic about the equality word. Long term, though, I think things will be better. Because the younger generations are more embracing of differences than their elders.

"How about advice for me these days?"

"I love men, by the way. Women do not think less of men if they hang out with minorities. We *want* you to be a guy. But always be a gentleman. No matter how much a young person rolls their eyes.

Practice being a gentleman. This 'everything has to be 50/50' is a joke. Just be yourself."

Alison goes on. "Here are three of my rules and advice for men."

1. Tell the truth. Even if it gets you in trouble.

2. Give back to society in some way.

3. Don't call older people by their first names. Have respect.

"Wow," I said. "You really like men."

"Men are everything," Alison said to me. "They remind us that we're women."

CUT THROUGH THE CRAP.

45 | THE ACTRESS

I had a several-year love affair with Hollywood in the mid-1970s. I was hired by an independent movie producer to write an original screenplay based on a wildly best-selling book, *The Money Game*. The book had no storylines. It was a book rehashing the writer Adam Smith's columns in the *New York Herald Tribune*. It was full of Wall Street characters and they are excellent. But no storyline. I had written, in 1972, a very successful book, *Confessions of a Stockbroker*. The producer read it, saw my photo on the back jacket, and decided "this guy wants to be in showbiz."

While I was in Los Angeles working on this original screenplay for *Money Game*, another producer surfaced out of the blue, interested in optioning one of my books. His name was Harry Gittes, also an independent producer, very well-known in Hollywood for his sense of humor and his strong friendship with Jack Nicholson. The hero, played by Jack in *Chinatown* was named J.J. Gittes. Harry and I met for dinner at a classic Hollywood restaurant, Musso & Frank, where the waiters had all worked there forever and the showbiz folks loved the ambience. With him that night was a date, the actress Gail Strickland. She was a hard-working pro, appearing in many movies, including costarring with Paul Newman in *The Drowning Pool*. I thought she was both very smart and funny. Before I left them after dinner, Gittes said to me, "You like her better than me."

It was tough not to like Harry. But Gail Strickland jumped out at you. When they stopped seeing each other I fixed her up with a friend of mine in Boston, who was thinking of relocating to LA. He was a big-time real estate developer. He and Gail met and, for the moment, fell in love. I knew that whatever happened, she and I would be lifelong friends. And we are. That romance soured but I didn't want her out of my life.

It's been said that Americans all have two jobs, their own ... and their love for show business. So if you're lucky enough to have an actress for a buddy ... embrace it. After a long courtship, Gail married another friend of mine, someone who had been my young summer camper when I was a junior counselor. I do believe that part of the good life is having friends who go back to childhood. It's wonderful for all involved, and it keeps you centered on times that were precious.

I counsel many young people. Years ago, recent college graduates knew they wanted to have a New York work experience. It was a rite of passage, like confirmation or losing your virginity. For the last twenty years or so, I've noticed that Los Angeles ... Hollywood, has replaced New York on the wish list of the young. So many millennials heading to LA.

Gail told me many pieces of wisdom I could pass on to all of my young correspondents.

"Cut your teeth in the theater ... on a stage," Gail says. "This is how a young person should begin to act, particularly acting in Manhattan. Other cities have great regional theater; Chicago,

Boston. But Hollywood, for all its glamour, is immature in certain ways, impressionable. Hollywood thinks *real* acting is on the stage, not on the screen. So many producers I've known think that if you've worked on Broadway, you're a *real* actor. When I first came to New York, I was 22 years old and had gotten into the acting class of Sanford Meisner. Of course, it changed my life. Here's my list of things that you should have tattooed somewhere if you want to act."

Gail went on a riff:

1. You have to want it more than all the other people who want it too.

2. Have enough financial security so you're not scared. Desperation is not your friend ... ever. This might mean bartending or waiting tables or family support.

3. Do three things every day to get an agent. Never, never, never be sexually vulnerable, to anyone for anything.

4. Short men can be tricky; it's not *you*. Knowing that helps.

5. Smile first, memorize, dress the part. Never send a video audition you are not committed to. Make a choice and own it. They want you to be better than what they thought they wanted. Understand that hair color, height, endless unknowables can eliminate you. That's what "don't take it personally" means. A sense of humor is your best friend ... always.

"Oh, and never *not* be taking classes, in something fun when possible. I took trapeze, wandered off in the canyon of La Cienega somewhere for lessons. Sometimes we actually peed in our tights, laughing. And we learned the thing. Came away with a resumé highlight, and a friend for life. Study the craft *all* the time, you will be practicing. It's essential. Much will be what *not* to do, very valuable. You will build a family of unique, like-minded friends, life saving.

"Always say *yes*, give yourself the opportunity for that to be the right answer. Pornography excluded. Nudity? You'll know.

"Early days in New York, a couple of jobs, sassy, an audition for a commercial something, had me climbing five flights to a cloistered room. There was an empty desk, and a balding, middle-plus aged man who smiled and was familiar. As I sat facing him … of course, he was the Maytag repair man, a wonderful character actor, Jesse White. My assumptions and naïveté about being a successful working actor, kinda famous, spoke in a rush, 'You still have to do this?' I blurted. With soft eyes looking right through to my panic, he responded, 'Yeah, sweetheart, that never changes.' The receptionist appeared, maybe twenty-three, first job, and curtly summoned, 'Jesse, you can go in now.' He winked at me as he headed off to try to get the job. It hadn't occurred to me that I would be auditioning the rest of my life.

"Dressing for a part gives me a big piece of how I see a character. For TV you need to be locked and loaded from the door. They don't have the time to inform and don't want to have to direct. One day there were six of us waiting to read, all similar physically, similarly dressed. Then a blonde walked in with that 'but I am blonde' confidence. That and an open vest, the sleeves of her blouse were perfectly rolled up three-quarter inches with the collar up, further creating a relaxed assurance. We were, all of us, buttoned up in blazers. I knew immediately she was right. The girl ahead of me went in and I popped into the bathroom. I hung my blazer in a stall, rolled up my sleeves, brushed my shiny red hair and, hearing my name, waltzed into the studio without looking back. When I returned she had buttoned her vest rolled down her sleeves and collar, so, not so confident. I forgot the blazer but got the part.

"For my third and final callback for *The Drowning Pool*, the director Stuart Rosenberg and producers David Foster and Larry Turnan were requiring me to let them see me in underwear. A pivotal scene, Lou Hopper and Mavis Kilbourne attempting to escape an airtight room filling with water and then stripping and stuffing the clothes in the drain. I understood why, and I was willing. But how would that happen? Alan Shane, the casting director, only offered 'do whatever makes you comfortable.' Every scenario seemed ridiculously embarrassing for all of us. I had to make them laugh. A naïve thirty-year-old auditioning for a strip club, badly. I borrowed a $400 Pucci bikini from friend Susan Blakely (gorgeous model/actress), got a recording of strip music. I showed up in a three-layer outfit including winter hat and scarf. I walked in mute giving no explanation with an anxious, too-big smile and looked for any place to perform. A wingback chair offered the only privacy for the finish ta-da! I placed the recorder on the floor, hit play and executed an insanely awkward, well-rehearsed strip. I ducked behind the chair for the last reveal uttering my only word, 'shit,' letting them guess why, and rose like a desperate Phoenix, arms flaying in search of an appropriate pose. I had them with the music. Gathering my pile of clothes, I backed out the door, closed it gently and sat in the hall reveling in the wild laughter. Alan went into the room, came back immediately and pulled me to my feet beaming. I had the part. I think I got most of my parts leaving them laughing.

"When I had been acting for 25 years, I lost my voice. Oh, I could talk ... but haltingly. I couldn't get the words out. It was dysphonia, diagnosed as a condition that doesn't get better. I tried to fake it as my world came tumbling down. After a while I couldn't hide it from anyone. In 1983 Ed Zwick offered me the lead in *Special Bulletin*, a news anchor tracking a terrorist incident in real time. I'd gotten through rehearsal barely covering a breathless voice.

"The first day filming was just me, the whole part was speaking directly into the camera, I was undone. Ed, his partner, their wives, all producers just behind the camera, wanting me to be brilliant. By lunch I knew it was beyond me and asked to be released. But I struggled on until they found a replacement, Kathryn Walker. I drove out to the marina and climbed into bed with Neil, my husband. I sobbed telling him my career was over. And it was. Twenty-one years later in 2003, I was cast as Sandra Day O'Connor in *First*

Monday in October. They ultimately looped my entire part in the pilot with another actress, without telling me. Being looped was the most embarrassing, demoralizing experience of my life. The show was not picked up. I told my agent I was done.

"How did I manage to continue working never knowing if I would have a reliable voice? Job after job, showing up camera ready and usually sleep-deprived, and terrified. I developed tricks, changing octaves, pushing difficult words, making being understood the driving energy behind an acting role. I went to the only speech therapist who worked with this disorder. Partnered with O.J. Simpson for two sessions in a workshop. He was scared as well, we bonded ... OMG. The years of stress, fellow actors needing me to repeat my lines, kind sound people whispering in my ear not to worry they would fix me ... OMG. Looping for hours! Trying to repeat lines endlessly.

"Retiring was a relief in that regard. Our daughter Maisie was nine, had a learning issue and getting her through school became my career. I cooked lunch and dinner for a women's homeless shelter in Santa Monica four days a week. Hosted fundraisers, gave so many dinner parties, went to P-town for long, spoiled summers. And then read a memoir story for a group in Hollywood. I introduced my disorder, Spasmodic Dysphonia, explained it could fuck me up, got a huge laugh, and was seduced. Having won an audience, was as close to being reborn as a failed Baptist would get in this life. I have produced nine Provincetown Story Nights. It has become an anticipated community event, a word-of-mouth sell out. I invite five local people to join me in writing and reading a memoir. I have created a place for myself to show off, to feed my appetite for the joy of performing."

Everyone reading this should pay attention to one of the big themes of the pandemic: reinvention. It takes guts to reinvent, particularly if the greatest love of your life, acting, is ripped away from you. More than any other profession, acting comes with rejection. It also comes, more than any other profession, with sexual challenges in the workplace. Gail had her own 'Me Too' experience but was not part of the many women who came forward to call him out.

"We met at Hefner's mansion in Chicago, a ridiculous place swollen with luxury and barely clad Bunnies to point the way to all manner of fun. It was 1972. Everyone was famous or young and pretty. He was famous, I was not. He knew Heff was producing a film directed by Donald Driver. He had not seen a play written and directed by Mr. Driver at the Ivanhoe theater but wasn't I the 'brilliantly reviewed leading actress?'

"'Well, I'm ... '

"'You're on the brink of a great career Gail ... It's Gail, right? Why don't you come to LA on your day off, I'm shooting a film there and I'll introduce you to ... ' They could have been football players or interior decorators, all I heard was 'Come to Hollywood, I know PEOPLE!' Canvassing my castmates, all hungry for a break, it was unanimous.

Oh my God you have to go!

What an opportunity, this is your chance!

Don't hesitate he might change his mind!

Can I come? I'll do your hair and make up.

You lucky lucky duck!

"David Wilson, my costar, took me to the airport after the Sunday matinee. He gave me a good squeeze at the gate and as he walked away threw a 'watch out, kiddo,' over his shoulder.

"'David, wait, watch out for what?' He waved but did not break stride. Watch out for all the wonderful opportunities, that's what I decided and smiled at the first class stewardess asking for my menu choice. The ticket had arrived by messenger, it required my signature.

"'Are you Gail Strickland? I'm Lester, I'm going to deliver you to him. Do you have any baggage?' Lester was an ex-football player, a huge person with giant hands and a limp. He spoke without nuance. He opened the rear door, but said he was okay with me sitting up front with him. As we crested the 405 at Mulholland Drive, the valley below twinkled a Disney welcome. It was a small room with a shallow stage. The piano, bass, guitar, and drums were crowded. The man was playing the drums. Did I know he played jazz drums? Lester pointed to a front row table, 'That's his table.' Then Lester was gone. The base was mid riff of something I'd later said was a favorite, I lied, I knew nothing. I hated jazz. The drums came in for a hot finish, he could play drums. Seeing me, he flashed that money grin and hopped off the stage still holding his sticks. He dusted the top of my head with a kiss and reached for my hand as he sat. 'Welcome to Tinsel Town, what are you drinking?'

"'A Coke with lemon, please, they gave us champagne on the plane.'

"The cozy two-story 1940s cabin, a charming rental, back over the hill tucked in off Benedict Canyon. The guest room was just to the right of the massive, heavily carved front door and angry gargoyle. Kinda weird. He put my suitcase on the bed and then led the way to the kitchen where we made peanut butter and grape jelly sandwiches washed down with a cold glass of milk. He was first on the call sheet, Santa Monica beach, 6 a.m., we would need to leave by 5:30 if we wanted to see them blow up the helicopter … And we did.

"'The producers always show up for the explosions.' He would introduce me to them and the director who was already casting his next movie. 'Gail, there is a part you'd be perfect for.' Again that pursed lip smile with gentle, hooded eyes as he said good night at my door. We missed the explosion, the producers and then there was never the right moment to meet the director. No worries, Lester would bring me by tomorrow on the way to the airport. Better day for introductions, no explosions. Fading light brought a wrap. Early dinner watching Monday Night Football was the plan for the evening as he had a 4:30 call in the morning. After a quick cold shower, boy, I was sunburnt, I joined him upstairs in the master suite.

"A sitting room with high beamed ceiling, walk-in stone fireplace burning sweet-smelling something, a sunken Jacuzzi bubbling an invitation and a huge TV at the end of a king bed. The game was on, dinner waiting under silver domes. The room vibrated with warm perfection. I devoured the sublime lamb chops, medium rare, how did they know? Baked-twice, stuffed potato ... really, and a Caesar salad sans anchovies, a given? Embroidered linen napkins in a 1966 Château Lafite Rothschild, I couldn't speak. He did not speak while eating and watching the Bears and who cares. Fine, as I owned no vocabulary for football. At halftime I took the dishes to the kitchen, whoever made dinner left it spotless. I returned to find him propped on the bed, stripped to his boxers with a bowl of ice between his legs. 'Come on up here, I'll cool off that burn.' Oh David, here's the *watch out.*

"I sat on the edge of the bed. He slid over and began to unbutton my blouse. 'Thank you but I think another cold shower is best.' Then he grabbed my arm. I pushed him hard in the chest freeing myself, then fell to the floor. He followed close, berating me as I took the stairs two at a time. 'You stupid fucking cow, who do you think you are? You're not pretty enough to say no.' That was his final shot before my slamming the door. I locked the door, I locked the bathroom door. Sitting on the toilet sobbing, leaking snot, stinging head to toe with sunburn, I wrote a pathetic apology on fifteen pages torn from my journal. Both sides. I wrote the last sentence in French, what was that about? *Je suis très, très désolé pardonne moi s'il vous plaît.* I wrapped all of my cash, $176, in toilet paper stuffed that and the fifteen pages in the envelope my ticket came in. On the outside I wrote 'I will send you the rest.'

"I woke up to pounding on the door. I had fallen asleep dressed for travel. Lester was yelling we had to leave for the airport. I sat in the back, numb. Now, decades later, as the women who have been drugged and raped by that monster come forward, I feel like a lucky, lucky, lucky duck. The luckiest."

I keep learning "true grit" from Gail. She is determined every day to squeeze that lemon of life dry. To get up every day with purpose and go on stage. Hit your marks and you smile at yourself in the mirror. And, like Roy Scheider in *All That Jazz*, say into the mirror ... *It's showtime!*

YOU WANT AN ACTING CAREER?
YOU'D BETTER BE TOUGHER THAN ANYONE ELSE.

46 | THE COUNTESS

I'm ending this journey through my education over a lifetime with a return to the past and a woman who had a big influence on my life on many levels. I always called her "the Countess." She was the widowed mother of two of my college friends who grew up in Manhattan, in an apartment at the very end of East 69th Street. It was where the city meets the East River, and the noises of boats at night made you feel in your dreams that you were at sea. The Countess' apartment always made me think of Never-Never Land. A place for boys who refused to grow up.

The first time I stayed in the Countess' place I awoke on a Saturday morning with the kind of hangover that has you saying silent prayers. Prayers about how you will never do certain things again in your life, if only the headache and the upset stomach will disappear. I lay in a twin bed in one of her son's rooms. It was 10:30 in the morning, and he hadn't even made it home from the night before. We were going to graduate from college in the spring, and we thought there wasn't *anyone* who deserved good times more than we. The Countess burst into the bedroom carrying a tray laden with scrambled eggs, English muffins with Keiller's Dundee marmalade, orange juice and black coffee.

"You know," she said, "you really are good fellows. Why do you make such dreadful asses of yourselves?"

That was the last thing I wanted to hear that morning. But the first thing I *did* want was what was on that breakfast tray. I sat up eagerly, arranging the covers so the tray might fit comfortably over my lap. The Countess sat down on a chair at the foot of my bed. She deliberately picked up the glass of orange juice and drank it down. Then, as I watched, she attacked the eggs and English muffins. "It's about time you started planning for graduation," she said between bites. "From now on, never expect that the world owes you a living. Chester Bowles (an American diplomat), told me years ago about success in life. 'Success is not the result of good looks or brains or even money,' he said. 'Success is the result of perseverance.' I always remember that."

She finished her coffee. The eggs and muffins were gone. She got up and left her tray on the chair. "You can take a shower now," she said, leaving the room. "And you may take my dishes to the kitchen and wash them, dry them, and put them away."

Now this, I thought, was a lady of leisure. She was 75 years old. She was elegant and beautiful. But what she had just done let me know, at a critical time in my life, that the world did *not* owe me a living, that there will come a time when I was going to have to fend for myself.

After that incident, the Countess became as much a friend of mine as her sons were. She was one of the first to teach me the value of perseverance, and another major lesson as well—the secret of quitting as a winner, of not outstaying success. Her story is worth telling since she had put a special stamp on pieces of 20th-century history.

The Countess has filled her years with achievement and service. She grew up in Philadelphia where her parents were artists and musicians, both players in the Philadelphia Symphony. The Countess was a child prodigy on the violin, playing concerts all over Europe, several times on the same program as the great Paderewski. He called her "Sunshine."

"He would play the piano, practicing until his fingers bled," she told me. "That was when he was the finest pianist in the world. That was a lesson to me. But I stopped playing the violin seriously after World War I, when Poland was destroyed by the Germans. My parents were Polish, and I think my inherent seriousness about helping others comes from their efforts on behalf of the homeland. I was brought up in a patriotic tradition, a tradition that assured you help people less fortunate. I suppose I've been a true liberal all my life, at least until that term began to imply a certain fuzzy thinking. It was love of people that made me become an actress. I did a lot of club shows in Philadelphia, and I guess people noticed me. Winthrop Ames, one of the biggest Broadway producers of the day, sent a limousine to pick me up when I was 18. He was a friend of my parents and, I suppose, trying to gently discourage me. He took me to the Winter Garden Theatre, just off Broadway, and took me onto the empty stage. Very dramatic.

"'You have been gently nurtured, my dear,' Ames said. 'Only tough peasant flowers can survive in the theater.'

"That was a challenge," she said. "For the next seven years I was on the stage, finishing in New York opposite Freddie March who was a friend until he died. During that period I was also in six silent films, including several with Mary Astor, Augie Perkins, and Glen Hunter." She laughed. "I was very big in *The Life of Anne Hutchinson*, shot on the old sound stages in Astoria, New York."

The Countess was one of the famous beauties of her era. She went to parties on the Lido in Venice with Elsa Maxwell. She was a guest at Gerald and Sarah Murphy's in Cap-Ferrat when Scott Fitzgerald threatened to dive naked off the cliffs into the sea. She flew upside down in a biplane piloted by Harry Crosby, co-founder of the Black Sun Press in Paris, over the Harvard-Yale boat race in New London, and she sang after hours in bistros with Josephine Baker in the Paris of the Lost Generation.

"I participated," she told me, "yet I was always the observer. Most of the notorious people of that time were like children, sweet, innocent, self-destructive children. Harry Crosby sent me violets every day for a year. Fitzgerald would pinch me and see if anyone was looking. I think that, because my parents took me to destroyed Poland each year when I was a little girl, I grew up knowing that one had to give life a purpose, but the most important pursuit in life was in preserving an innate seriousness that said, 'Give of yourself.'"

She left the theater at a time when directors called daily and scripts flowed to her apartment at the rate of 30 a week. "There became too much self-absorption in the acting profession," she told me. "Lorette Taylor was the greatest actor I ever saw. She could fill a stage with panic. But the drinking ... So self-destructive. I seem to know instinctively when I've had enough of anything, even though with the theater I was like a war horse smelling gun powder. The discipline it has taught has allowed me to survive loneliness, disappointment, unhappiness. Discipline in the theater is the most important element, discipline that rivals that of West Point."

Most of my meetings with the Countess were on the beach where we both had spent our summers. She rallied on the tennis court with one son for half an hour early in the morning. Then she read and wrote letters. I saw her on the beach where she brought her lunch and held a salon under a striped umbrella. Over the years, her themes remained the same: optimism about the human condition and the sense that self can overcome obstacles.

"I had a feeling years ago," she told me, "Hemingway was a desperate man and would destroy himself. So much talent I've seen in this century turned to alcohol and eventual suicide. Dorothy Parker, I remember, tried to kill herself unsuccessfully. Bob Benchley, the humorist, wrote her a note saying, 'Stop it. You'll ruin your health.'"

When the Countess' husband was killed in World War II in the OSS, she became instrumental in organizing UNICEF at the United Nations. "Everything that happened in the war ... I felt that saving children was the key to the future. But not just saving lives, catering to people's stomachs. I felt our job was bigger than that. How to motivate people so they can live better lives."

Part of what makes a warrior, to me, is the degree to which they fight one of America's biggest diseases: loneliness.

"Loneliness is particularly hard for women today," said the Countess. "I never remarried. I cope with loneliness in several ways. I read books. I go to the theater. I stay close to friends I have known for years. I pay attention to detail, which is everything in being successful. The big picture is made up of many small details. Above all, and this is more important than any element in building a life that makes sense, *I listen to what people say.* Most of us don't ever listen to others; our egos get in the way. We don't want to get involved. When I am interested enough to hear someone else, I get results. Eugene O'Neill thought I was a wonderful woman. I acted in Provincetown in 1923 and he brought fresh eggs to the theater to make me omelettes after the performance. 'Fresh eggs for the throat and the physique,' he would tell me. He always had a bottle of whiskey for himself, never to share. I'd eat some of the omelette and listen to him talk until it was time to go home."

The Countess could always listen. Her lesson to me is what draws people to her. They cannot believe a beautiful grande dame will bother listening to *their* story. She lived in New York until she died in 1987, in the same apartment where the boats go by in the night. When last I saw her on the beach that summer, I asked if she were finally ready to give up on New York in exchange for the country.

"Are you serious?" She asked me. "With more excitement than any city in the world? They've been talking about problems in London and Paris. God, London and Paris have been breathing their last for *centuries.*" I had lunch with her on the beach that summer. She drank iced tea and ate small cucumber sandwiches, with slices of cantaloupe covered in fresh lime juice for dessert. Several people joined us. The Countess always has attracted an entourage. People loved to be seen with her. Perhaps the special places, the memories will rub off on *us*. An assistant curator at a Texas museum came by, a senior editor of *Readers Digest*, an heir apparent at Citibank all came to sit at her feet. I often worried about where our country was going, what the future would bring. I wanted to be reassured. We all asked the Countess questions.

"The problem with America," she says, "is that we haven't suffered enough. In 1958 I came back from touring Asia for UNICEF. I felt I was coming back to the Roman Empire. We had so *much*. We do not learn from history. H.L. Mencken called us 'boobus Americanus' and I often think that's so accurate. Are we bound for perdition?" Taking a bit of cantaloupe, the Countess continued, "We've gotten so far away from religion. So much of 'I, I, I,' is all we hear. The shibboleths of our culture are no longer supported by science. We've licked the natural forces, and we can't believe in mystery any more. Science and technology have become the opiate of the people. Much to their sadness, I'm sure. If you could strip away the glee over impending Disc-O-Vision and a better detergent, we'd all be better off. We have to search for new identity to overcome the spiritual blankness. But whatever the research will produce, they'd better hurry." This was in 1980. She stood up and adjusted her wide brimmed hat so that the sun would not dare violate her cheeks. "I'm going home to write letters," she announced, "while you children can 'fleet the time carelessly as they did in the golden world.'" She drops lines like these as if she were born to make entrances and exits written by Shakespeare expressly for her. Rosalind, in *As You Like It*, had been her favorite role.

She handed me her used paper plate. Nothing was left on it but crumbs and lime juice. "Dump this for me, please?" she asked, reminding me of that time years ago when I was hung over and did her breakfast dishes. "You have to be reminded, no matter how old you get—never coast on your charm."

She walked across the sand to her car, a 1962 Bentley that had 140,000 miles on the odometer and that she always drove herself.

Her granddaughter is the great comedic actress, Téa Leoni. Téa now owns her grandmother's house where she wanted her two kids to be raised in the summers, to understand the roots of the place.

Téa's most recent role was the lead in the CBS series, *Madame Secretary*. She is a longtime board member of UNICEF and, like her grandmother, cuts to the chase, and gets to the heart of the matter.

I left the wisdom I got from the Countess for the last chapter. It took me back to the past and lifted me into the present and future, living next to Téa Leoni in the summertime. Téa is the logical keeper of her grandmother's flame.

The biggest lessons of all I've learned from these important women in my life, are epitomized by the Countess and her granddaughter. These are what I hope men can learn and pay attention to much more than they do now:

> LISTEN TO OTHERS.
>
> BE OPEN MINDED TO NEW EXPERIENCES AND OPINIONS.
>
> BE TOLERANT.
>
> TRY TO SOLVE PROBLEMS BY ASKING YOURSELF: "HOW WOULD A SMART WOMAN APPROACH THIS?"

If you pay attention to these things, you will have a more thoughtful and rich and interesting life.

Give it a whirl.

ACKNOWLEDGMENTS

My appreciation goes to the special team at TidePool Press who acquired and produced this book and who love books with a passion—it's apparent in their work. They love the process. They love the craft. It's less a business, more a pleasure. So, with all that in mind, I thank TidePool's Jock Herron, Ingrid Mach, Frank Herron, Dany Pelletier and Linda Chadwick for the care and diligence they put into this project.

And I wish to acknowledge my long-time agent and friend John Taylor (Ike) Williams.

And I must give special thanks to my son, Nick, who drew and designed the cover and created the cartoon inside. He is a director of TV commercials and a staff cartoonist for *The American Bystander* magazine.

OTHER BOOKS BY JOHN D. SPOONER

Fiction

The Pheasant-lined Vest of Charlie Freeman:
A Novel of Wall Street (1967)

Three Cheers for War in General: A Novel of the Army Reserve
(1968)

Class (1973)

The King of Terrors (1975)

The Foursome (1993)

Nonfiction

Confessions of a Stockbroker (1972)

Smart People: A User's Guide To Experts (1979)

Sex and Money: Behind the Scenes with the Big-Time Brokers
(1985)

A Book for Boston (1980)

Do You Want To Make Money Or Would You Rather
Fool Around? (1999)

No One Ever Told Us That – Money and Life Letters to
My Grandchildren (2012)

No One Ever Told Us That – Money and Life Lessons for
Young Adults (2015)